B. H. P. Fisher

# ST BASIL THE GREAT

## A STUDY IN MONASTICISM

CAMBRIDGE UNIVERSITY PRESS
London: FETTER LANE, E.C.
C. F. CLAY, Manager

Edinburgh: 100, PRINCES STREET
Berlin: A. ASHER AND CO.
Leipzig: F. A. BROCKHAUS
New York: G. P. PUTNAM'S SONS
Bombay and Calcutta: MACMILLAN AND CO., Ltd.
Toronto: J. M. DENT AND SONS, Ltd.
Tokyo: THE MARUZEN-KABUSHIKI-KAISHA

# ST BASIL THE GREAT

## A STUDY IN MONASTICISM

BY

### W. K. LOWTHER CLARKE

FORMERLY FELLOW OF JESUS COLLEGE, CAMBRIDGE
RECTOR OF CAVENDISH, SUFFOLK

Cambridge :

at the University Press

1913

𝔆𝔞𝔪𝔟𝔯𝔦𝔡𝔤𝔢 :

PRINTED BY JOHN CLAY, M.A.

AT THE UNIVERSITY PRESS

FILIOLO MEO BASILIO

a 3

# PREFACE

THE early history of monasticism has attracted much attention in recent years, and the labours of such scholars as Butler, Ladeuze, Preuschen and others have thrown a flood of new light on the subject. This is especially true of Egypt, which was for a whole century the Holy Land of organised asceticism, and has claimed quite properly the first attention of scholars. But there remain fields of importance which are as yet comparatively unworked, foremost among which may be mentioned the movement inaugurated in Cappadocia and Pontus by St Basil. So far as I am aware, there exists no account of the ascetic writings of the great archbishop of Caesarea, that discusses their contents and problems with any fulness of detail. And yet St Basil forms an important link in the history of monasticism, and deserves more consideration than he has received hitherto. I trust that the present study may do something to fill the gap.

My main purpose has been to make a careful examination of St Basil's *Ascetica*. I have not however confined myself to this; it is difficult to understand any subject in isolation, and so, at the risk of going once more over ground already well trodden, I have tried to put my account of the literature into a historical framework, and, in particular, to compare Cappadocian monachism with the systems that existed in Egypt in the first half of the fourth century, and the subsequent institutions of both East and West. The conclusions reached with reference to the literature cannot claim to be anything more than provisional, in the absence of a proper critical edition of the Basilian Rules. The general lines of the picture are not however affected by the uncertainty of the textual problems, and the main result of the book—that the spiritual sons of St Basil are to be found in the Western rather than the Eastern Church—agrees with the verdict of most recent writers on the subject.

I have derived little help from the modern *Lives* of St Basil, and have formed my conclusions in the main from an independent study of the ascetic writings. The Benedictine edition, by Garnier and Maran, has been constantly at my side; although nearly 200 years old, it is still a treasury of learning and critical insight; while Maran's *Life of St Basil*, prefixed to the third volume, is almost equally valuable. I have used the 1839 edition, which is better printed and more convenient to handle than Migne's later edition. The fullest account of the Rules seems to be that of H. Leclercq in his article "Cénobitisme" in the *Dictionnaire d'Archéologie chrétienne*. A book by A. Kranich, *Die Ascetik in ihrer dogmatischen Grundlage bei Basilius dem Grossen*, is, as its title indicates, concerned with the doctrinal rather than the practical side of the question, and does not attempt to institute comparisons with other types of asceticism. The footnotes and Bibliography should show with sufficient clearness what books have been consulted. In common with other workers in this field, I owe much to the writings of Dom E. C. Butler, and in particular to his chapter on Monasticism in the first volume of *The Cambridge Medieval History*, with its full and discriminating bibliography. Two books on special points have proved more than ordinarily suggestive—Loofs' *Eustathius von Sebaste* and Holl's *Enthusiasmus und Bussgewalt*. For the later history of Greek monasticism Ph. Meyer's *Die Haupturkunden für die Geschichte der Athosklöster* is still the most valuable guide. Wherever possible, standard translations have been used, especially those of the *Nicene and post-Nicene Fathers* series, the original being given in a note if demanded by the importance of the point at issue.

I have to express my gratitude to Mr H. G. Wood, late fellow of Jesus College, Cambridge, for reading my manuscript and suggesting some improvements and corrections; also to the Professors of Divinity at Cambridge University, who have been good enough to accept my dissertation as a sufficient exercise for the degree of Bachelor of Divinity.

Since writing the above Mr E. F. Morison's book on St Basil has come into my hands (*St Basil and his Rule*, Oxford, 1912). It is a curious coincidence that two students should have been at work independently upon a subject hitherto untouched by English scholars. On most points I find myself in complete agreement with Mr Morison. In the few cases where we differ an examination of his views has not led me to alter my own conclusions, and I have therefore contented myself with giving references to the relevant pages in his book.

W. K. LOWTHER CLARKE.

*June* 14, 1913.

[Feast of St Basil—Western Church.]

# CONTENTS

# CHAPTER I

## ASCETICISM IN THE EARLY CHURCH

FEW movements in the religious sphere have received such unsympathetic treatment in the past at the hands of English writers as those ascetic tendencies of the early Church which found their expression in monastic institutions. The late Mr Lecky described the movement in these words: "There is, perhaps, no phase in the moral history of mankind of a deeper or more painful interest than this ascetic epidemic. A hideous, sordid, and emaciated maniac, without knowledge, without patriotism, without natural affection, passing his life in a long routine of useless and atrocious self-torture, and quailing before the ghastly phantoms of his delirious brain, had become the ideal of the nations which had known the writings of Plato and Cicero and the lives of Socrates and Cato[1]." Dr Inge, speaking of the development of the Church, can represent "the ascetic and monastic movement" as "the strangest aberration in its history[2]." Of late, however, partly owing to the wide influence of Dr Harnack's writings[3], a more sympathetic spirit has prevailed. It is now generally recognised that an ideal which has enlisted in its service so many of the best of humanity, and played so important a part in the forming of the nations of modern Europe, deserves more respectful treatment.

In the fourth century A.D., there lived a number of great personalities, whose careers have a permanent attraction for the student of history. Prominent among these is St Basil of Caesarea; even during his life-time his reputation was

---

[1] *History of European Morals* (ed. 1911), II. 107.
[2] *Truth and Falsehood in Religion*, p. 163.
[3] *Monasticism* (Eng. tr. 1901), and *What is Christianity?* pp. 242 ff.

wide-spread, and after his death he ranked as one of the greatest saints and doctors of the Eastern Church. He was conspicuous as a preacher and skilful administrator, his theological writings were an important factor in the eventual triumph of Nicene orthodoxy; yet his main title to fame is his work as a founder of monastic institutions. As such he is a figure of considerable importance. He is revered to-day as the originator of the monasticism of the Eastern Church. If we reflect on the vast resources of the Russian Empire, the contributions which it has already made to the world's culture in the fields of music and literature, and the part that it will probably play in the history of the near future, we shall be led to pay serious attention to Eastern monachism, as one of the dominating forces in the Russian Church. The fact that Russian bishops are chosen from the monastic clergy is sufficient in itself to show the significance of monasticism. Recent events have reminded us that the Greeks and the minor Slavonic nations are in the full flush of a renascence in which the various national Churches will be called upon to take their part.

But St Basil and his work come nearer home to us than this. During the early Middle Ages the Benedictine monks were one of the greatest spiritual and civilising influences of Western Europe, and through St Benedict St Basil has touched the West. According to Dom Butler, " St Benedict owed more of the ground-ideas of his Rule to St Basil than to any other monastic legislator[1]." St Basil is therefore one of the outstanding figures in the history of monasticism, and in the following pages we shall try to estimate the value and permanence of his work.

Before attacking this special problem it will be well to put one or two questions with reference to the general subject. What, we may ask, is meant by asceticism? Was it of Jewish or pagan origin? Did Christ inculcate or even countenance it in His teaching? How came it to permeate the Church so completely? After briefly discussing these

[1] *Enc. Brit.* (11th ed.), art. "Basilian Monks" (all subsequent references are to this latest edition).

points and sketching the development of the ascetic ideal during the first three Christian centuries, we shall be in a better position to appreciate the mental presuppositions of an educated Christian in the fourth century.

The word "asceticism," like many other words, is used in both good and bad senses. It is sometimes interpreted as connoting a rigorous maltreatment of the body, arising from a Manichean conception of the evil of material things. But we have not disposed of a thing by calling it Manichean. The Manichean position is after all but an exaggeration of an essentially religious attitude. It is no doubt truer to place the root of evil in the will, but for practical purposes the average man finds his flesh the greatest obstacle to the attainment of virtue, and all the higher religions have made energetic provision for the curbing of the flesh[1]. However, the best exponents of Christian asceticism would not allow that material things are evil in themselves, for, as St Basil says, God would not have made them, had this been the case. They would only claim that the man who would be holy must attain a mastery over the material, and that he will do this rather by despising than by using it.

It is fairer to frame a definition that does not beg the question. *The Concise Oxford Dictionary* defines an ascetic as "one who practises severe self-discipline." If we add a proviso that asceticism is severe self-discipline undertaken for religious ends, and that the discipline will be exercised with reference both to the natural desires of the body and the distractions of the outer world, we have a definition that will suit our purpose[2]. No reasonable man will quarrel with this principle of discipline. Self-expression and self-restraint are two equally essential elements of religious life. In order to

---

[1] It is worthy of notice that the modern view of sin, which finds its essence in the survival of animal instincts which were once natural but now conflict with man's higher life, has considerable affinities with the ascetic position.

[2] Heimbucher's definition may be cited as a specimen of a Roman Catholic view: "eine planmässig geordnete und beharrlich fortgesetzte fromme Lebensweise, verbunden mit freiwilliger Entsagung von dem, was nach dem christlichen Sittengesetze zwar nicht verboten ist, aber dessen Enthaltung durch die evangelischen Räte als besonders gottgefälliges Werk bezeichnet wird." *Die Orden und Kongregationen der katholischen Kirche* (1896), p. 31.

live in the world at all, it is necessary to use the world ; but anyone who attempts to use it to the full must expect spiritual deterioration.  But when we proceed to ask how far asceticism is a necessary constituent of religion, or to what extent the severity should be carried, we find ourselves on debatable ground, where there is room for legitimate differences of opinion.  In particular there are a number of practices which have existed in non-Christian societies, but have been presented to the European observer mainly through the agency of Christian monasticism.  Chief among these may be mentioned abstinence from marriage on religious grounds, renunciation of private property, and, less essentially characteristic, the rendering of absolute obedience to the will of another[1].  It may be argued that these practices have proved disastrous to the higher life of Churches and nations, or that the ideals enshrined in them have been exaggerated out of all proportion, but no one could say that they are in themselves other than a legitimate exercise of individual liberty.  Even in renouncing his own will the monk has not on the face of it done more than the soldier to whom he is often compared by the fourth century Fathers[2].

Assuming then that asceticism is best defined in neutral terms, we now ask how this tendency came to be so sharply emphasised in the Catholic Church of the fourth century. How, for instance, was it possible for a writer like Jerome to indite that terrible letter to Eustochium on Virginity, in which he describes motherhood in the most repulsive terms, and can only find one palliative of marriage, that without it virgins cannot be produced[3]?

To obtain an answer to this question we must go back to the beginnings of Christianity.  Christianity was of course far more than the mingling of the streams of Hebraism and Hellenism—otherwise Philo might have founded the Church.

---

[1] The threefold vow of Poverty, Chastity and Obedience is not however primitive.  In the rule of St Benedict there is a threefold promise of *stabilitas*, *conversio* (*morum*), *obedientia* (c. 58).

[2] St Basil works out the comparison in detail in his *Praevia Institutio Ascetica*. See p. 74.

[3] *Ep.* 22.

But it seems true to say that the human personality of Jesus Christ, the Founder of Christianity, was the finest flowering of the genius of the Jewish race, and that the particular form assumed by the Catholic Church was conditioned by the current Graeco-Roman civilisation of Mediterranean lands[1]. To which of these two elements, the Jewish or the pagan, is asceticism to be ascribed?

There need be little hesitation in affirming that the Jewish spirit as a whole was not ascetic. In early times it was believed that prosperity was an outward sign of the Divine favour. The experiences of the Exile shattered this simple faith, and the book of Job is the classical treatment in Jewish literature of the perplexities that ensued. But even after the Exile asceticism never found an entry in any true sense. It is surprising how little trace there is of it in the last three centuries B.C., especially when we consider that Persian dualism has left a distinct mark on the later books of the Old Testament; the practical conclusions that might have followed from a dualistic theology were apparently not drawn. Generally speaking, the Jew continued to have a keen relish for the good things of life, and accepted them gladly as God's gifts. Marriage was and always has been the duty of the adult Jew. The astonishing numbers of the Jews in the early Christian centuries must be attributed partly to the fact that the race honoured and practised matrimony in a world that was growing weary of it[2]. Nor was the Jew attracted by poverty; on the contrary, he was always alive to the possibilities of worldly advancement.

To this general statement of the case certain exceptions must be made. In the legal codes of the Old Testament

---

[1] Cf. Harnack's definition of Catholicism, "It is the Christian preaching influenced by the Old Testament, lifted out of its original environment and plunged into Hellenic modes of thought, i.e. into the syncretism of the age and the idealistic philosophy." *Constitution and Law of the Church*, p. 254.

[2] Of course only partly. Cf. Schürer, Hastings' *D.B.* v. 91, "It was not only to migrations and natural reproduction, but also to numerous conversions during the Greek period, that Judaism owed its wide diffusion over the whole world." Harnack, *Expansion of Christianity*, I. 10, lays stress on the conversions from kindred Semite races.

there are some ascetic injunctions, which may however be
plausibly explained as survivals of primitive taboos. Of more
importance is the quasi-ascetic life lived by individuals and
families during many centuries of Hebrew history. Its
purpose was to revert to the traditional simple life of the
desert, as a protest against the temptations to apostasy
arising from the Canaanite customs which were connected
with agriculture. The Nazirites and Rechabites are the chief
representatives of this tendency, but many of the prophets
shared the same views. Elijah and Amos especially were
prophets of the desert type. In New Testament times there
are some few indications of an ascetic tendency among the
Jews. The Essenes and Therapeutae are generally quoted
in this connexion. But they seem to have been syncretistic
sects, influenced by Hellenistic ideas, and have little bearing
on Judaism properly so-called. Dr Schweitzer has warned
us[1] of the false impression that we get of Jewish eschatology
in the first century A.D., when we leave out the two most
significant figures, Jesus Christ and John the Baptist. Similarly in the present connexion, these two are the most
important witnesses for first century Jewish asceticism. We
shall return presently to the witness of our Lord, but the
Baptist deserves a word here. He was, apparently, unmarried
and lived an ascetic life in the wilderness. Clad in the
traditional garb of the prophets of old, he preached to the
crowds who sought him in his retreat, and urged a faithful
performance of everyday duty. Besides these hearers he
had a number of disciples in a special sense of whom very
little is known. It is clear then that the Baptist is a characteristically Jewish figure, standing in the line of the prophetic
tradition, which has little in common with the later Christian
conception of asceticism. After the fall of Jerusalem great
changes took place in Judaism, which now provided more
congenial soil for the growth of the ascetic spirit. " The
destruction of the Holy City—" says Mr Box, "and above all
of the Temple—in 70 A.D., gave rise to a widespread ascetic

[1] *Quest of the Historical Jesus*, p. 366.

movement among the Jewish people who survived, especially in Palestine[1]."

If asceticism, as displayed in the Catholic Church, is not a product of Judaism, where it was only a late appearance of secondary importance, is it to be traced to the Gentile environment which modified the primitive Christian community so profoundly? There is much in favour of this view at first sight. The Greeks and Romans had not been ascetically inclined in their best days. But in the early years of the Empire nearly all earnest religious strivings assumed an ascetic form. The old national faiths proved inadequate amid the changed conditions, and men's eyes turned eastward. With the mixing of nationalities came a mixing of religions, and the Oriental cults with their promise of purification met the needs of a world in which moral earnestness had awakened to new life. The priests of Isis and Serapis, Cybele and Attis, were to be found in all the big cities, celibates of both sexes abounded, and, apart from the official priesthoods, wandering devotees, proclaiming each his own way of salvation, penetrated into the remotest districts[2]. Now these Eastern religions were definitely ascetic in their aims and methods. It is an obvious deduction that Catholic asceticism was a Gentile perversion of the original pure deposit of Christianity. And yet such a conclusion would be in the highest degree superficial. It is singularly difficult to substantiate any actual borrowing from pagan sources, and the true solution would seem to be on quite different lines.

We are driven therefore to seek an origin for Christian asceticism in the original deposit of Christianity. Asceticism seems to be present potentially in all religions, and makes its appearance in the higher religions, as soon as the child-like simplicity of primitive races has been replaced by some measure of introspection. In some nations, the Jews for instance, it plays little part; amongst others, such as the

[1] *The Ezra-Apocalypse*, p. 209. Note the emphasis on fasting (IX. 24) and chastity (VI. 32).

[2] Reitzenstein, *Die hellenistischen Mysterienreligionen*, p. 11. Cumont, *Les religions orientales dans le paganisme romain* (2nd ed.), p. 34 and *passim*.

higher races of India, it is almost identical with religion itself. The specific forms which asceticism assumed in the Church during the first four centuries after Christ may well have been conditioned by the existing state of society, but the thing itself was inherent in Christianity from the beginning. It could hardly have been otherwise, seeing that the Church was composed of men and women of a certain stage of civilisation, who were obviously children of their own time. Let us now attempt to trace the primitive Church conception of asceticism.

We have grown accustomed to a certain clearly-defined picture of Jesus Christ, such as is presented to us in modern literature and art. We see Him moving about in the towns and villages of Galilee, sharing the life and joys of common people, looking at the world with fresh, unspoiled interest, as if it had come straight from the Father's hand, loving birds, flowers, mountain-tops and little children, seeing, both in the operations of Nature and the social relationships of human life, analogies to the dealings of God with souls. The correctness of part, at least, of this impression is guaranteed by the fact that contemporary observers dubbed Him "gluttonous and a wine-bibber." And so we find it difficult to sympathise with the Church Fathers, when they see in Christ the typical ascetic. And yet there is much in the Gospel presentment of Christ's teaching and example that accords with this interpretation. Our Lord lived a virgin life in a land and among a people where marriage was well-nigh universal. His example was reinforced by direct teaching, as when he speaks of men becoming eunuchs for the sake of the Kingdom of Heaven[1], or of the call to hate wife and family for His sake[2], or when He describes the angelic life as one in which there is no marriage[3]. It would be a mistake to underrate the social

---

[1] Mt. xix. 21. It is not necessary to investigate the meaning of this and other passages as originally spoken. It is sufficient for our purpose to show that the ascetically minded could appeal to the recorded life and teaching of Christ in support of their position.

[2] Lk. xiv. 26, xviii. 29. In Mk x. 29, Mt. xix. 29 "wife" is absent from the best texts. See Burkitt, *Early Eastern Christianity*, pp. 119, 120.

[3] Mk xii. 25, cf. Lk. xx. 34, 35, where the heightening is marked.

rank of Jesus and His disciples, yet it is clear that they were poor during the travels of the Ministry. The Son of Man had not where to lay His head. The utmost simplicity of food and clothing was enjoined on the disciples. The rich young man was bidden to part with all his possessions and follow Christ, and, according to St Matthew, this was represented as being, for him at least, the perfect way[1]. In fact Western Christianity has never really faced the full implications of Christ's teaching on poverty and riches. Jesus is represented as having fasted Himself, and having contemplated the continuance of the practice by His followers[2]. And, generally speaking, the precepts about cutting off the hand or foot and plucking out the eye readily lent themselves to an ascetic interpretation.

The above is sufficient evidence of the existence of ascetic traits in the earliest strata of Christianity. But the question as to the real meaning of Christ's teaching is of such interest that a few words must be given to its consideration.

What has been said above with reference to John the Baptist is also applicable here. Our Lord stands, as regards the external conditions of His ministry, in the line of the prophetic tradition. During the greater part of His public career His work was to proclaim the nearness of the coming Kingdom and the necessity of repentance as a preparation for it. In the opening verses of St Mark we find Him taking up and reinforcing the Baptist's message[3]. It was only to be expected that His own life, in certain aspects, should recall the desert type of prophet. In so far as the disciples shared His life, it was necessary to prescribe for them a similar detachment from worldly ties. The practical necessities of evangelism will thus have dictated the ascetic precepts of the gospels[4].

True as this argument no doubt is, it seems, to the writer at any rate, not strong enough to bear the full weight of the

---

[1] Mt. xix. 21, Mk x. 21, Lk. xviii. 22.

[2] Mt. iv. 2, vi. 16, ix. 15, Mk ii. 20.    [3] Mk i. 14, 15.

[4] Cf. *Didache*, 11, where the apostles and prophets seem to be classed together as travelling evangelists.

evidence. There is more in Christ's words than these considerations can explain. An alternative solution of the problem is offered by what has been called *Interimsethik*.

According to this theory[1], the key to the teaching of Jesus, especially in the Sermon on the Mount, lies in the fact that it was never intended for a permanent rule of life, but only for the brief period that was expected to end presently in the passing of the existing world-order. If this be granted, the ascetic precepts become intelligible at once, and form an integral part of an "anti-family and anti-social" teaching[2].

The strength of the arguments in favour of the eschatological view is not to be ignored, but it is difficult to imagine that such an interpretation is much better than a caricature of Christ's ethical demands. "The theory gives a low and unworthy colouring to the teaching of Jesus, since it represents Him as laying the whole stress on the self-centred desire of the individual for his own salvation, and as caring little or nothing for the effect of good actions on others and the world as a whole[3]." Besides, there are a number of passages which support a different conclusion and indicate that Jesus looked forward to a prolonged absence[4]. They are an integral part of the Synoptic tradition[5], and are in fact so opposed to the general Church sentiment of the first decades that their authenticity is indubitable. We conclude that the ascetic precepts are no *Interimsethik*, but are part of a body of teaching adapted to the needs of Christ's followers during a period of indefinite prolongation.

Jesus then recognised a life of asceticism as necessary for some of His followers, in view of the requirements of the Gospel preaching or the needs of individual souls. There is no evidence that He required it from all, or that He made it

---

[1] Expounded by J. Weiss, *Die Predigt Jesu vom Reiche Gottes*, and Schweitzer, *The Quest*.

[2] Felix d'Alviella, *Évolution du Dogme Catholique*, p. 33 (quoted by Emmet, "Is the teaching of Jesus an Interimsethik?" *Expos.* Nov. 1912).

[3] Emmet, *loc. cit.*

[4] Mt. xxv. 5, Lk. xii. 45, xix. 11 ff. Cf. also the parables of the Wheat and Tares, Mustard Seed, and Leaven, which contemplate a period of slow growth.

[5] See the index references to the above passages in *Oxford Studies in the Synoptic Problem*.

a general condition of perfection. But if individuals in later times have heard an inward voice calling them to a life of celibacy and hardship, they have not misinterpreted the Gospel story by recognising in it the Spirit of Jesus.

It may be objected that the world-renouncing side of Christ's teaching is a secondary and quite subordinate element. This may be the case; we are not claiming that the conclusions of the early Church were valid for all time, only that the interpretation, so far as it went, was legitimate. It seems impossible for any one age to appreciate the totality of Christ's message; it must suffice if it carry away such lessons as it can assimilate.

Asceticism is represented in other writings of the New Testament besides the gospels, but it is entirely practical in its aims. It may be summed up in the words "No soldier on service entangleth himself in the affairs of this life[1]." The writers are convinced it is the last hour; the world and its lusts are passing away[2]. It is only common-sense that Christians should desire to go through life as far as possible without *impedimenta*. Moreover, idolatry permeated every department of pagan society, and the command "Keep yourselves from idols[3]" was equivalent in practice to "Renounce the world." St Paul in places goes further than this, for instance in his teaching about marriage in 1 Corinthians. "I cannot see how it is possible to deny," says Professor Lake, "that the general teaching of the Christian Church from St Paul to the Reformation is that the life of the celibate is higher *qua talis* than that of the married Christian[4]." That is to say, the Catholic view of marriage was no innovation, but a logical if one-sided development of a point of view that is firmly entrenched in the New Testament. The early Church in its idealisation of the unmarried state, and its resolve to flee from the world rather than realise itself in the world, could appeal to its canonical documents[5].

---

[1] 2 Tim. ii. 4.

[2] 1 Jn ii. 17, 18.     [3] 1 Jn v. 21.     [4] *Earlier Epistles of St Paul*, p. 191.

[5] The "virgins" in Rev. xiv. 4 are most significant; some commentators however give them a symbolical sense.

It is outside our scope to discuss the development of ascetic ideals in the ante-Nicene Church; all that is really germane to the subject will be introduced more fitly in Chapter III under the head of the origin of Egyptian Monasticism. It will be sufficient at this point to give a summary statement of the facts. In the third century certain precursors of the later monks make their appearance. They are not however of much significance and, with the exception of the philosophical schools of Alexandria, do not seem to have had any organic connexion with the movement inaugurated by St Antony[1]. More important for our purpose is the custom, practised by devotees of both sexes, of leading an ascetic life at home without separation from other Christians. This was described as bearing "the whole yoke of the Lord[2]." " No doubt now existed in the Churches that abstinence from marriage, from wine and flesh, and from possessions, was the perfect fulfilling of the law of Christ[3]." The extreme ascetic position was however condemned as heretical, and the fact that asceticism was most fully developed in the Gnostic and Catharist sects might well have rendered it suspect in the eyes of the adherents of the great Church, had not its presuppositions been common ground to all professing Christians.

Can we account for the strength of this conviction that the ascetic is the true Christian? We have seen that the first generation of believers looked for a speedy return of Christ, an expectation which, coupled with the necessities of the missionary propaganda, led many of them naturally to set

---

[1] The following may be mentioned: (*a*) Origenistic ascetic schools, e.g. those of Pierius and Hierakas; (*b*) the wandering ascetics of the pseudo-Clementine epistles on Virginity; (*c*) the "monks" referred to in Eusebius, *Mart. Pal.* 5. 10, *Comm. on Ps.* 67 (68); ("The first order of those who are pre-eminent in Christ is that of the monks; but they are few") 83 (84); (*d*) the "sons of the covenant" found in Aphraates, *Hom.* VI. XVIII. See Zöckler, *Askese und Mönchtum*, pp. 174—182.

[2] *Didache*, 6.

[3] Harnack, *History of Dogma*, I. 238. See 1 Clem. 38, Ign. *ad Polyc.* 5. ("In these ascetics of early Christianity the first step was taken towards monasticism," Harnack, *Expansion of Christianity*, I. 272). Just. *Apol.* I. 15. Clem. Al. *Strom.* VII. 12. Tert. *de Virg. vel.* 10. *Apol.* 9. Cypr. *de hab. virg.* 3 ff.; cf. Herm. *Mand.* IV. 4, *Sim.* V. 3.

small store by earthly relationships. As years passed by and the second Advent was still unrealised, the expectation was perforce weakened. The best spirits of the Church did not however settle down to make the best of the present world. The political and social conditions of the time were not favourable to such a development. The persecutions alone were enough to keep alive the original feeling towards the world. And so the asceticism of the apostolic days, begun on practical grounds, was continued for the same reasons. Now it frequently happens that men are led by the force of circumstances to adopt a certain course of action, and only after they have pursued it for some time do they seek a theoretical justification for their behaviour. Such seems to have been the case here. The Church writers found asceticism an established fact in their midst and sought to explain it as a necessary deduction from Holy Scripture. In so doing they emphasised certain elements of New Testament Christianity out of all proportion and destroyed the balance preserved in the apostolic writings. But their explanations are after-thoughts and only to a very limited extent correspond to the facts of history.

No single cause is sufficient to account for the great proportions assumed by the ascetic movement in the fourth century. The ideal had been present in the Church from the beginning in germ, and a desire to imitate the life of Christ literally, and obey his precepts, continued to be a factor in the situation. But fourth century monasticism on the scale on which we know it was only made possible by a number of causes which combined to foster the ascetic ideal. The three cardinal virtues of monachism—virginity, poverty, and obedience to a spiritual guide or a written rule—presented few difficulties to the men of the time. Marriage was not attractive. The natural human desire for a wife and family has seldom been so weakened as at this epoch. The decline of the population cannot be attributed merely to a vicious fiscal system. Racial decay was undoubtedly present, while slavery had produced its inevitable crop of moral and physical deterioration. Nor did poverty possess much terror for the

better class of citizens.   There were few or no openings for a
young man in political life, and the exactions of the Exchequer
made existence almost intolerable to many citizens.   Rarely
have the charms of the simplified life and freedom from the
burden of responsibilities proved so alluring.   Again, the last
thing that the Empire wished to encourage in its sons was
independence or initiative.   The spiritual fatigue of the time
made it no hardship for the average monk to transfer the
control of his actions to some masterful abbot such as
Pachomius or Schnoudi.

Many circumstances thus prepared the way for monasticism, but it would be a mistake to lay too much stress on
social influences.   In any great religious movement, as M.
Cumont points out[1], we come in the last resort to a series of
individual conversions, for which moral causes must be sought.
The moral factor here is not far to seek, namely, the changed
conditions that ensued on the cessation of persecutions and
founding of the Christian Empire[2].   A flood of new members
swept into the Church and swamped the old landmarks, the
standard of Church life deteriorated sensibly, and earnest
spirits craved for new opportunities of holiness.   These they
sought in the cell and cloister; there was no longer any call
to withstand the forces of the pagan Empire, but in the desert
the martyr-spirit found a new expression, and there was scope
for any amount of moral enthusiasm in spiritual conflicts with
the powers of darkness.   Monasticism then in one of its
aspects was a protest against the growing secularisation of
the Church, which had ceased to be a community of saints
and was now a school for righteousness with many reluctant
pupils.   With the monks enthusiasm revived, and the pioneers
at least were conscious of possessing supernatural gifts and
powers.   The monks may even be called Puritans, and it is

---

[1] *Les religions orientales*, p. 41, "Une grande conquête religieuse...ne s'explique
que par des causes morales.   Quelque part qu'il faille y faire, comme dans tout
phénomène social, à l'instinct d'imitation et à la contagion de l'exemple, on
aboutit toujours en définitive à une série de conversions individuelles."

[2] The great development of monachism coincided with the Christian Empire,
though its beginnings were of course earlier.

one of the surprises of history that they were preserved in communion with the world-Church.

Even now we have not accounted for the phenomena of the fourth century. Much is explained, but not the irresistible impulse, almost madness, which swept over great tracts of country and drove so large a proportion of the population to a life of incredible austerities. But it is just in this that the fascination of history lies; the student feels himself confronted by forces too mighty to be measured by any instruments at his disposal.

# CHAPTER II

## THE CHILDHOOD AND YOUTH OF ST BASIL[1]

It is usual to begin the biography of a great man with some account of the family from which he sprung and the surroundings of his childhood. Such preliminaries must not be omitted here, for in Basil's case both heredity and environment played a clearly-defined part.

His native land Cappadocia[2] is an upland plain occupying the central part of Eastern Asia Minor. Several mountains rise up from the plain, the most important being Mt Argaeus (now Erjish Dagh). The climate is of a continental character, being subject to great extremes of temperature. Sozomen remarks on "the severity of the winter, which is always a natural feature of that country[3]," and Basil mentions it several times in his correspondence. The soil is naturally poor, but generations of working peasants had brought it to moderate fertility at a time before historical records begin[4]. This district had once been the seat of the Hittite empire, and it is probable that the Hittite racial type persisted in Basil's time. "With the decline of the Syro-Cappadocians after their defeat by Croesus, Cappadocia was left in the power of a sort of feudal aristocracy, dwelling in strong castles and keeping the peasants in a servile condition, which later made them apt for

---

[1] Excellent *Lives* of Basil are given by Venables in *Dict. Chr. Biog.* and Jackson in his translation of Basil in the *Nicene Fathers* series. Maran's *Life* in the Benedictine edition is the fullest. Allard's *Saint Basile* (5th ed. 1903) is delightful from a literary standpoint, but superficial. There are also popular works by Fialon (1861) and R. T. Smith (1879). Tillemont's *Mémoires* are still useful.

[2] See art. "Cappadocia" in *Enc. Brit.* (11th ed.).

[3] *H.E.* VI. 34. Cappadocia was noted for furs, *Camb. Med. Hist.* I. 548.

[4] Sir W. M. Ramsay, *Luke the Physician*, p. 179.

foreign slavery[1]." The national reputation was bad, and Cappadocians ranked with Cretans and Cilicians as an unsatisfactory trio[2]. Gregory of Nyssa tells us that the Cappadocians were poor in almost everything and especially in men able to write[3]. Amid these peasants were a number of "farmsteadings of quadrilateral shape, having at the four corners, towers, which were connected by walls and inner chambers, enclosing an open quadrangle....In those big fortified homesteads lived the large patriarchal households of the landholders, representatives of the conquering caste in a subjugated land....From those landed families came some of the leading figures in early Church history, such as Basil of Caesarea[4]." The main lines of these "Tetrapyrgia" are followed in the still existing Seljuk Khans[5].

In striking contrast to the backwardness of the imperfectly Hellenised country folk stood the brilliant civilisation of Caesarea. According to Strabo only Mazaca (Caesarea) and Tyana among Cappadocian towns deserved the name of city[6]. In 260 A.D. Caesarea was said to contain 400,000 people[7]. It rose to wealth and importance as the manufacturing and business centre of a large province almost destitute of towns[8]. There is no reason to think that Gregory is using language of indiscriminate patriotism when he speaks of the literary distinction of Caesarea, and calls it "this illustrious city of ours...the metropolis of letters, no less than of the cities which she excels and reigns over[9]." Caesarea then was

[1] *Enc. Brit.* art. "Cappadocia."
[2] Καππάδοκες Κρῆτες Κίλικες τρία κάππα κάκιστα.  [3] *Ep.* 12.
[4] Ramsay, *Luke the Physician*, p. 187; cf. Cumont, *Les religions orientales*, p. 213, "Sous la domination des Achéménides, l'est de l'Asie Mineure fut colonisé par les Perses. Le plateau d'Anatolie se rapprochait, par ses cultures et son climat, de celui de l'Iran et se prêtait notamment à l'élève des chevaux. La noblesse, qui possédait le sol, appartenait en Cappadoce et même dans le Pont, comme en Arménie, à la nation conquérante."
[5] For a photograph see Ramsay, *op. cit.* p. 192. Cf. Greg. Nyss. *Ep.* 15, for a description of a country mansion.
[6] *Enc. Brit.* art. "Cappadocia."   [7] *Enc. Brit.* art. "Caesarea."
[8] Soz. *H.E.* v. 4. For Caesarea as a centre of the road-system see the maps of Asia Minor in Ramsay's books and Hastings' *D.B.* v., also Miss Skeel, *Travel in the First Century*, pp. 124 f.
[9] Greg. Naz. *Or.* 43, 13.

L. C.

a centre of Greek influences in a district where the old native ways of life still predominated. The final process of Hellenisation was carried out by the Church rather than the State, and Basil and others like him, who were equally at home in city life and on their country estates, were important agents in the process. Pontus, the other province with which Basil's family was associated, was a land of high mountains, deep valleys and rushing streams, with a winter climate even more severe than that of Cappadocia.

Christianity had taken root in Cappadocia from early days. The Jews who abounded here, as elsewhere in Asia Minor, formed a nucleus for the Church[1]. Asia Minor, so Dr Harnack reminds us, was "the Christian country κατ᾿ ἐξοχήν during the pre-Constantine era[2]," and Cappadocia did not fall short of its neighbours. After making due allowance for patriotic rhetoric, we may still regard Gregory of Nyssa's words as remarkable: "If it is really possible to infer God's presence from visible symbols, one might more justly consider that He dwelt in the Cappadocian nation than in any of the spots outside it. For how many altars are there, on which the name of the Lord is glorified! One could hardly count so many altars in all the rest of the world[3]." Gregory's testimony is corroborated by the fact that Julian found Cappadocia a stronghold of Christianity; nor are there any but faint traces of heathenism in Basil's writings. This part of Asia had great Christian traditions. One of the most noteworthy of third century bishops, Firmilian the friend and correspondent of Cyprian[4], had been associated with Caesarea, and an even greater figure, Gregory Thaumaturgus, had been bishop of Neo-Caesarea in Pontus[5]. Cappadocia, unlike its western neighbour Phrygia, had been comparatively free from heretical tendencies, and this added prestige to the metropolitan church of the province. The archbishop of Caesarea was of course head of the Cappadocian Church; his position

---

[1] 1 Macc. xv. 22 (see Schürer, *The Jewish People*, II. ii. 221), Acts ii. 9, 1 Pet. i. 1.  In the two latter Pontus is mentioned with Cappadocia.
[2] *Expansion of Christianity*, II. 326; cf. 338—353 for Cappadocia.
[3] *Ep.* 2.                                   [4] Cypr. *Ep.* 75.
[5] See Harnack, *Expansion*, II. 349—352, for the significance of Gregory.

was the stronger in that the bishops of the province were few in number and the towns over which they presided, with the exception of Tyana, of little importance[1]. He claimed metropolitan rights over Pontus and Lesser Armenia, and the great personal influence of Basil enhanced the already high reputation of his see.

Basil came of a family that had won honourable distinction for its steadfast devotion to the faith. His paternal grandfather was a landed proprietor near Neo-Caesarea, who had fled with his wife Macrina into the wilds of Pontus to escape from the persecution of Maximinus[2]. His father Basil, an eminent member of the Bar at Caesarea and a teacher of rhetoric, married Emmelia, a woman of great force of character and deep religious fervour. Both father and mother came of illustrious families which had given a long line of officials to the State[3]. In all their children there appears an ease of bearing and power of administration, which stamp them as belonging to the aristocracy of the district[4]. Gregory remarks of Basil's paternal grand-parents how great a trial their exile was to them, since they were "accustomed to the attendance and honour of a numerous retinue[5]." Basil *père* and Emmelia showed much generosity in their extensive charities, and dedicated to God a fixed proportion of their property, which was still large in spite of losses during the persecutions[6]. They had ten children, of whom four sons and five daughters survived. Macrina the eldest lived to become one of the most remarkable women of the century, and her *Life* by her brother Gregory is a fascinating record that deserves to be better known. The other four daughters were all happily married. Basil was the eldest son; next to him came Naucratius, who

---

[1] Cf. Duchesne, *Histoire ancienne de l'église* (1907), II. 378. The institution of village-bishops (χωρεπίσκοποι) on the contrary was highly developed.

[2] Greg. Naz. *Or.* 43, 5—8.     [3] *ib.* 3.

[4] Rufinus, *H.E.* II. 9, describes Gregory Naz. and Basil as "ambo nobiles"; cf. Allard, *Saint Basile*, p. 2, who draws attention to their love of nature : " ce sentiment de la nature, cet amour de la campagne, qui est, à sa manière, une note d'aristocratie, et ne se rencontre guère chez des hommes nouveaux, n'ayant point de racines dans le sol."

[5] Greg. Naz. *Or.* 43, 3.     [6] *ib.* 9.

was killed on a hunting expedition in Pontus. Gregory and Peter, the two youngest sons, became eventually bishops of Nyssa and Sebaste.

Basil was born about the year 329, apparently at Caesarea[1]. His health as an infant was frail, and he was put out to be nursed with a family in the neighbourhood, who were paid by the gift of the usufruct of some slaves[2]. When he was strong enough, he was sent to his grandmother Macrina to be brought up on the family estate at Annesi, near Neo-Caesarea. Macrina gave him his first lessons in religion; she was in touch with the traditions of the time of persecution, and could repeat to the intelligent boy the very words used by the great Gregory Thaumaturgus[3]. Thus early in his lifetime did Basil come under the influence of the Origenistic tradition. His father seems to have been teaching at Neo-Caesarea about this time, for Gregory relates, " In his earliest years he was swathed and fashioned...under his great father, acknowledged in those days by Pontus as its common teacher in virtue[4]." This training under his father may have been contemporaneous with that received at the hands of Macrina. " He was trained in general education, and practised in the worship of God, and, to speak concisely, led on by elementary instruction to future perfection[5]." It was to his father that Basil owed the foundations of his liberal education and wide culture. His sister Macrina had been educated very differently and debarred from pagan literature, while on the death of their father she herself undertook the education of the youngest brother Peter, which she conducted on severely ascetic lines[6]. The time now came for Basil to leave home. " When sufficiently trained at home...he set out for the city of Caesarea, to take his place in the schools there[7]." We have already mentioned the literary distinction of Caesarea, and Basil would have received there as good an education as

---

[1] See Greg. Naz. *Ep.* 2; Bas. *Epp.* 51, 74, 76, 87, 96, all of which refer to Cappadocia or Caesarea as his native place. There is however no direct statement.

[2] Bas. *Ep.* 37; cf. Greg. Nyss. *in laud. Bas.*          [3] Bas. *Epp.* 204, 210, 223.

[4] Greg. Naz. *Or.* 43, 12.          [5] *ib.*

[6] Greg. Nyss. *Vit. Macr.* (*P. G.* XLVI. 961 ff.).          [7] Greg. Naz. *Or.* 43, 13.

a provincial city could give[1]. He made rapid progress, and
won a reputation by his prowess in philosophy and rhetoric[2].
It is possible that he met Julian and Gallus during this period,
for about this time they were confined in the palace of Ma-
cellum not far from Caesarea. The correspondence between
Basil and Julian is however of doubtful authenticity. The
famous friendship between Basil and Gregory must have
started at Caesarea. "Athens...brought me to know Basil
more perfectly," says Gregory, "though he had not been
unknown to me before[3]." After finishing his course at
Caesarea, Basil went to Constantinople, where he met the
famous champion of an expiring paganism, the rhetorician
Libanius, and profited by his instructions[4]. Constantinople
"was distinguished by the eminence of its rhetorical and
philosophic teachers, whose most valuable lessons he soon
assimilated[5]."

From Constantinople Basil proceeded in 351 to Athens.
He found that his friend Gregory had reached the University
city a little before him, after travels in search of education
that had extended as far as Palestine and Alexandria[6].
Perhaps this example led Basil eventually to visit the same
countries in search of a different kind of knowledge. Basil
found his early days at Athens far from happy. The rough
horse-play of the students, the "ragging" practised on fresh-
men and the rivalries of different nationalities caused great
annoyance to his sensitive nature, although he was spared
much by his friend's influence. However, the fascination of
studying under the best teachers of the age[7] soon out-balanced

---

[1] See Bas. *Ep.* 76; cf. Eus. *Vit. Const.* IV. 43, where the Cappadocian bishops
are described as "distinguished above all for learning and eloquence."

[2] Greg. Naz. *Or.* 43, 13.          [3] *ib.* 14.

[4] Libanius was in Constantinople about this time. The Libanius-Basil correspondence, *Epp.* 335—359, if not genuine, may have been inspired by a true
tradition of their intercourse. The statement of Socrates, IV. 26, and Sozomen, VI.
17, that they met at Antioch is no doubt due to a confusion with Chrysostom's
friend, Basil of Antioch. Libanius went to Antioch about 353. Cf. Seeck, *Die
Briefe des Libanius* (1906); Maas, *Der Briefwechsel zwischen Basileios und Libanios*
(1912).

[5] Greg. Naz. *Or.* 43, 14.          [6] *ib.* 7, 6.

[7] Himerius and Prohaeresius (Socr. *H.E.* IV. 26).

such inconveniences, and he became very happy. The two
friends found no time for anything but their religious duties
and their studies. "Two ways were known to us, the first of
greater value, the second of smaller consequence; the one
leading to our sacred buildings and the teachers there, the
other to secular instructors." Athens was a stronghold of the
old religions, but, unlike Julian, Basil does not seem to have
felt their attraction. He and Gregory led a life of devotion
and purity, and had no youthful sins with which to reproach
themselves, though no doubt their development up to this
time was one-sided and unduly academic. In spite of their
seclusion, Basil's qualities as a leader were manifested, and a
group of like-minded students gathered round the two friends.
When the time for parting arrived, about the end of 355, the
wrench was painful on both sides[1].

How had it fared meanwhile with the family that Basil
had left behind? About the time of his departure from
Caesarea his father died, and the responsibility for the younger
children and the scattered and extensive family property
devolved on Emmelia. The burden was however to a very
large extent borne by the eldest daughter Macrina, who had
vowed herself to life-long virginity on the death of her
affianced husband, which took place when she was twelve
years old. Gregory of Nyssa gives a full description of his
sister's life during these years, but leaves the chronology
obscure. He himself was still devoted to secular pursuits,
while Emmelia, Macrina and the youngest child Peter were
on the family estate at Annesi, living as ascetic a life as was
possible in view of their responsibilities[2]. About 352, so it
seems, Naucratius the remaining son began his remarkable
career of asceticism. He retired into the wilds of Pontus
some three days' journey from home, accompanied by a faithful domestic Chrysapius[3]. They found a retreat on the banks
of the Iris, and spent their days mostly in hunting and fishing.
Being highly skilled in the chase, Naucratius succeeded in

---

[1] Greg. Naz. *Or.* 43, 14—24 is our authority for the years at Athens. Cf.
Capes, *University Life in Ancient Athens.*

[2] Greg. Nyss. *Vit. Macr.* (*P. G.* XLVI. 965 ff.).

[3] *ib.* 968, πρὸς τὸν μονήρη καὶ ἀκτήμονα βίον ἀπῆλθεν.

getting more than was required for their own subsistence. He gave the surplus to the aged and sick men of the neighbourhood, to whose necessities he also ministered with his own hands. After five years spent in this "philosophic" life, the two died suddenly as the result of a hunting accident. Emmelia was prostrate with grief, and Macrina succeeded in persuading her mother to adopt a life of greater asceticism. This happened about 357, when Basil either had started, or was just about to start, on his travels in the East. The dates are not quite certain, but one would like to think that the tragic death of Naucratius was not unconnected with his resolve to forswear worldly ambitions. By this time the other four sisters were all married, and the family possessions distributed among the children[1].

Basil returned to Caesarea at the beginning of 356. His fame had preceded him, and the city "took possession of him as a second founder and patron," and claimed him as a teacher of rhetoric[2]. The citizens of Neo-Caesarea looked on him as one of themselves and, taking advantage of Basil's visit to his mother at Annesi, sent a deputation to invite him to become a teacher in their city[3]. But other influences were now at work. Macrina was alarmed at the developments in her brother's character. Though Gregory, the friend, denies it[4], Gregory, the brother, declares expressly that Basil's head was completely turned by his success[5]. But no doubt a desire for an ascetic life had been in his mind for a long while, though perhaps obscured of late by his brilliant achievements[6]. His

[1] Greg. Nyss. *Vit. Macr.* (*P. G.* XLVI. 969).

[2] Greg. Naz. *Or.* 43, 25. Rufin. *H.E.* II. 9; cf. Bas. *Ep.* 358 (Libanius to Basil—of doubtful authenticity).

[3] Bas. *Ep.* 210. The *Dict. Chr. Biog.* article speaks of two attempts to get him. But Basil must have visited his mother and sister (see *Vit. Macr.*), and in *Ep.* 210 he says to the Neo-Caesareans, "you were not able to *keep* me," so that Annesi is the natural background for this deputation. "Afterwards, when you all crowded round me, what were you not ready to give?" refers more naturally to the informal proceedings at the close of the deputation than to a second deputation.

[4] Greg. Naz. *Or.* 43, 25, "after a slight indulgence to the world and the stage, sufficient to gratify the general desire, not from any inclination to theatrical display."    [5] Greg. Nyss. *Vit. Macr.* (*P. G.* XLVI. 965).

[6] Greg. Naz. *Ep.* 1 speaks of a promise made by the two students at Athens

morals had always been irreproachable, and, as we saw in Chapter I, Catholic piety had manifested itself for generations past in ascetic forms.  The visit to his old home would awaken dormant memories, and the sight of its quiet and disciplined life stir him to new and higher ideals.  Besides this, Macrina made a direct attack on him, and the words of his revered sister went far to effect his conversion[1].  In *Epistle* 223 Basil gives us his own account of the change.  It was sudden, like a man awaking from sleep.  He wept over his wasted life, and the years spent in acquiring worldly wisdom.  He prayed for light, and found it in the words of the Gospel which bid men sell their goods and renounce the world.  And then he needed a guide, one who had already espoused the perfect way of life. "And many did I find in Alexandria, and many in the rest of Egypt, and others in Palestine, and in Coele Syria, and in Mesopotamia."

A little further on in the same letter he relates how he found men living the same life in his own country, clearly referring to Eustathius of Sebaste.  But in spite of this, which may be taken to mean that only after his return from the East did he receive instruction from Eustathius, it seems more likely that they met before his departure.  Eustathius had become bishop of Sebaste by 357[2], Sebaste was not far from Neo-Caesarea, Basil's family was connected with Sebaste, perhaps having property there[3], Eustathius had himself visited Egypt and Palestine—what is more probable than that Eustathius advised Basil to travel and learn the ascetic way for himself from a first-hand acquaintance with its exponents[4].  We recollect that Gregory of Nazianzus had visited

---

to join one another later on in a life of "philosophy."  For the different meanings of φιλοσοφία in Christian writers see Boulenger's note, *Grégoire de Nazianze, discours funèbres*, pp. lvi, lvii.  This writer's suggestion that Basil led a life "quelque peu dissipée" is not warranted by the evidence.

[1] *Vit. Macr.* 973.    [2] See *Dict. Chr. Biog.* art. "Eustathius."

[3] Greg. Nyss. *Or. in XL Mart.* speaks of Sebaste as the πατρίς of his forefathers.

[4] Cf. Duchesne, *Histoire ancienne de l'église* (1907), II. 384, "C'est sans doute sur les conseils de l'évêque de Sébaste qu'il entreprit un grand voyage en Égypte, en Syrie et en Mésopotamie, pour visiter, lui aussi, les solitaires les plus renommés."

the same lands, and so may have been an influence in the same direction.

Basil now returned to Caesarea[1], and put his worldly affairs in order, though his renunciation of his possessions cannot have taken place until after his travels, which must have been costly. Somewhere about this time he was baptised by Dianius, bishop of Caesarea, and ordained to the office of Reader[2].

We have singularly little information about Basil's journeys. He cannot have been gone much over a year, for we find him back at Caesarea in 358. He reached Egypt, his main objective, by way of Syria. After a halt at Alexandria, apparently occasioned by sickness[3], he traversed "the rest of Egypt[4]." He did not succeed in meeting the great Athanasius[5], and he avoided the company of heretics[6]. After Egypt he went to Palestine and Mesopotamia, and thus home to Cappadocia. This is his description of the effect produced on his mind by what he saw: "I admired their continence in living, and their endurance in toil; I was amazed at their persistence in prayer and at their triumphing over sleep; subdued by no natural necessity, ever keeping their soul's purpose high and free, in hunger, in thirst, in cold, in nakedness, they never yielded to the body; they were never willing to waste attention on it; always, as though living in a flesh that was not theirs, they showed in very deed what it is to sojourn for a while in this life, and what it is to have one's citizenship and home in heaven. All this moved my admiration. I called these men's lives blessed, in that they did indeed show that they 'bear about in their body the dying of Jesus.' And I prayed that I, too, as far as in me lay, might imitate them[7]."

What precisely was this life that Basil saw and determined to imitate? To answer this question will be the task of the following chapter.

---

[1] This is nowhere stated, but seems highly probable.

[2] Bas. *de Spir. Sanc.* 29; Greg. Naz. *Or.* 43, 27.

[3] Bas. *Ep.* 1. He declares here that his real object was to meet his correspondent, Eustathius the philosopher, but this is mere epistolary politeness. Cf. *Reg. brev. tract.* 254.     [4] *Ep.* 223.     [5] *ib.* 80.     [6] *ib.* 204.     [7] *ib.* 223.

# CHAPTER III

### EGYPTIAN MONASTICISM

THAT Basil should visit Egypt was only to be expected. Few countries have exercised so powerful an influence on the religious ideals of mankind as the lands which lie at the south-eastern corner of the Mediterranean. But Palestine was now politically extinct, and its importance for Christian circles in the following century was due to an antiquarian revival. Arabia's contribution to religious thought was still in the future. In Egypt however the intellectual side of later paganism had reached its highest development, and the Christian Church, stimulated perhaps by the vigour of its rival, had become famous both for orthodoxy and asceticism. Basil therefore devoted most of the time at his disposal to an investigation of Egyptian Monasticism[1].

In the earlier Egyptian documents there is no trace of the ascetic ideal. It is only in the sixth century B.C. that we begin to detect its presence. Its origin is a disputed question, but Professor Petrie thinks that Indian influences must have reached Egypt about this time, when north-west India was an important province of the Persian Empire, and that later on, when the Persian boundaries shrunk, such communications would have been interrupted[2]. Philo gives us a description, perhaps somewhat idealised, of the life led by ascetically-

---

[1] Cf. Duchesne, *Histoire ancienne*, II. 486, "L'Égypte était le sanctuaire de l'orthodoxie, la terre classique des confesseurs de la foi....Le pays où vivaient ces saints gens (les moines), où fleurissaient les institutions émanées d'eux, devint bientôt une seconde Terre-Sainte."

[2] Petrie, *Personal Religion in Egypt before Christianity*, p. 57; cf. Zöckler, *Askese und Mönchtum*, pp. 94—97; Wiedemann, *Religion of Egypt* (Hastings' *D.B.* v. 177 ff.).

minded Hellenistic Jews of both sexes in the first century A.D.[1]
There are indications that similar tendencies prevailed in
heathen circles during the first three centuries A.D. Certainly
there were many devotees of the heathen gods; there is however no trace of anything resembling a monastic community.
The data are at the best slight and obscure, and an elaborate
superstructure has been built on an insecure foundation. It
has been frequently stated that colonies of recluses living a
severe monastic life were attached to the temples of Serapis,
and especially to the Serapeum at Memphis. Dr Preuschen
describes the whole theory as a "castle in the air"; he considers that "recluse" is a wrong translation of κάτοχος,
"possessed" being the correct rendering. The people in
question visited the sanctuary in order to sleep on the spot
inhabited by the god. They were, so it was believed, possessed
by the god during sleep and received either a cure of their
sickness, or a dream-oracle revealing the means of health.
Various motives, such as poverty, or desire of notoriety, may
have caused the stay to be prolonged in some cases. In the
vast complex of buildings attached to the Serapeum there
were many occupations by which a living could be earned.
There are however no signs of any "cells," nor is there reason
to suppose that the temple was ever visited from motives of
penitence. It would seem then that Christian monasticism
was not, as far as our present knowledge goes, a copy of pagan
institutions[2].

---

[1] See Conybeare, *De Vit. Cont.*, for a defence of the genuineness of the
treatise, and parallels from undoubted works of Philo.

[2] Preuschen, *Mönchtum und Sarapiskult* (1903). See a full discussion by
Reitzenstein (*Die hellenistischen Mysterienreligionen*, pp. 72—81), who rejects
Preuschen's interpretation and gives evidence to show that the κάτοχοι were
*prisoners* of Serapis, that is, novices, who waited for years, sometimes all their
life, for initiation. He concludes however with Preuschen that there was nothing
resembling monasticism. "Mit dem Mönchtum hat diese Art Clausur...nur
insofern etwas zu tun, als sie eine Art Askese bedeutet." This idea among others
may have had an influence (*mitwirken*) in some monastic circles; "der ursprüng-
liche Sinn beider Institutionen ist dennoch verschieden" (80, 81). Even though
his words are only put in question form, it is most misleading if Professor Gwatkin
asks "whether some of the earliest Christian monasteries may not have been
heathen monasteries converted wholesale to Christianity, but continuing their old
rule of life with little or no change" (*Early Church History* (1909), I. 246). For

In Chapter I we have discussed the general conditions
which facilitated the rise of Monasticism. But why did it
make its historical appearance in Egypt rather than some
other country? If the attempt to find an answer in the
arrangements of the Serapeum at Memphis has failed, there
remains a more promising field of search in the Christian
and heathen philosophical schools of Alexandria. In spite
of confusion in the evidence it seems clear that the Neo-
Platonists and Christian Platonists were closely connected.
Ammonius Saccas, the founder of the Neo-Platonist School,
is said to have been originally a Christian[1]. Origen was one
of his pupils[2], and on becoming a teacher himself attempted
a synthesis on a grand scale between the Gospel and philosophy[3]. His rash act of exaggerated self-discipline is well
known; nearly all the leading ideas of later asceticism may
be found in his writings[4]. His influence was potent in the
later Church, and Basil and Gregory especially owed much
to him. So when we find the Gregories, in common with
other contemporary writers, calling monks philosophers and
asceticism the (true) philosophy, without comment or explanation, we naturally conclude that Origen's reconciliation of
the Church and philosophy was mainly responsible for the
conception. Here if anywhere, in the Christian philosophy
of Alexandria, must we look for the influence of heathen

the absence of the penitential element in native Egyptian religion see Budge, *The
Paradise of the Fathers*, I. xli; *Enc. of Rel. and Ethics*, III. 827a; Petrie, *Religion
of Ancient Egypt*, p. 89. The conclusion reached above does not debar us from
supposing that details of *ascetic practice* were borrowed, consciously or uncon-
sciously, from heathen sources.

[1] By Porphyry, quoted in *Dict. Chr. Biog.* art. "Ammonius Saccas."

[2] Eus. *H.E.* VI. 19.

[3] Cf. Bardenhewer, *Patrologie* (1910), p. 133, "In lauterstem Interesse um
der falschen Gnosis die wahre gegenüberzustellen und die gebildete Welt für die
Kirche zu gewinnen, unternahm es Origenes, die hellenische Philosophie mit dem
Glauben der Kirche zu verschmelzen. Aber sein vermeintlich christliches und
kirchliches Lehrsystem ist neuplatonisch und gnostisch gestimmt und getönt."

[4] This subject has been worked out by Bornemann, *In investiganda Monachatus origine quibus de causis ratio habenda sit Origenis.* See p. 8, "Illa
monastica disciplina, quam Basilius instituit, vix quicquam habuit, quod iam
saeculo tertio in ecclesia partum aut praeparatum non esset." He shows that
Origen emphasises the need of poverty, chastity, contemplation, retirement (of the
soul), and ascetic exercises (pp. 18—38).

ideas on the origin of monasticism. It is however better, as
we have already seen, to regard asceticism as belonging to
the stock of ideas common to all religions of the time, and so
inherent in Christianity from the first.

The Origenistic tradition was continued by the successive
heads of the catechetical school at Alexandria. Finally we
come to Hieracas, who lived at Leontopolis about the year
300. He carried some of Origen's tenets to an extreme and
heretical point, and collected round him a body of ascetics of
both sexes, who were probably out of communion with the
Church[1]. Dr Harnack says of him : " Hieracas is for us the
connecting link between Origen and the Coptic monks; the
union of ascetics founded by him may mark the transition
from the learned schools of the theologians to the society of
monks. But in his proposition that, as regards practice, the
suppression of the sexual impulse was the decisive, and
original, demand of the Logos Christ, Hieracas set up the
great theme of the Church of the fourth and following
century[2]." It is wiser perhaps not to attach much importance
to this sect, which is mainly known to us from one passage
of Epiphanius[3]; for by this time the true historical beginning
of monasticism had been already made, not amid the intellectual surroundings of Alexandria, but by unlettered Coptic
peasants.

The monks fall into two great divisions—the anchorites,
eremites or solitaries, whose names explain themselves, and
the cenobites, that is, followers of a "common life." In
describing the first class all three words will be used, but
only for the sake of variety; no difference in meaning is
intended. Where the mode of life borrows some features
from the cenobium, but is still essentially eremitic, it may be
termed semi-eremitic.

It was the general belief in the later Church that the
original form of monachism was cenobitic[4]. It was supposed

---

[1] Athan. *de Syn.* 16, seems to class Hieracas as a heretic.
[2] *History of Dogma*, III. 98, 99.
[3] *Haer.* 67, abridged by later authorities; cf. Butler, *Lausiac History*, II. 195.
[4] Cf. Cass. *Coll.* XVIII. 5.

to date back to the first generation of Christians at Jerusalem,
who had all things in common.   The Therapeutae, described
by Philo in his *De Vita Contemplativa*, were thought to be
Christian monks leading a common life.   Such ideas were
historically incorrect; the only ground on which it would be
possible now to uphold the priority of cenobitism is the
apparent existence of communities of women in the third
century.   In the *Life of Antony* we are told that the saint put
his sister in a nunnery (παρθενών) before retiring from the
world[1].   But this was not a cenobium in the later sense.   As
Professor Watson says : " In the days of St Athanasius there
were in Alexandria houses of virgins, though we must regard
these as substitutes for the home life and places where the
home life was lived.   In fact the monastic life for women
was first suggested by its proved success in the case of
men[2]."

If the solitaries were the first monks, the Decian persecution may have caused the adoption of the solitary life, as
tradition asserts.   Dionysius of Alexandria declares that a
number of Christians fled to the desert to escape from their
persecutors[3], and according to later writers some stayed there
when the persecution was over[4].   Paul of Thebes is said to
have been the first anchorite, but Jerome's *Life* of him is not
a good authority and must be regarded more or less as a
romance[5].   It is quite clear that there were ascetics before
Antony, for an old man living near his place of retirement
taught him the way of asceticism, and even in the early part
of his career he had sympathising companions[6].   But in spite
of all we may continue to call Antony the first monk.   To go
behind him in our search darkens the problem.   From the
days of Clement the ideal of a perfect Gnostic had existed,
but the important thing is not the existence of an ideal, but
its translation into life[7].   As Bornemann says with justice, the

[1] Athan. *Vit. Ant.* 3.          [2] *Ch. Quart. Rev.* Apr. 1907.
[3] Eus. *H.E.* VI. 42.          [4] Jer. *Vit. Paul.*; Soz. *H.E.* I. 12.
[5] The *Vita Antonii* is silent on the subject of Paul.
[6] Athan. *Vit. Ant.* 3, 4, 8, 11, 12.
[7] Cf. Holl, *Enthusiasmus und Bussgewalt beim griechischen Mönchtum*,
pp. 138, 139.

author of monasticism was not the first monk, but the first who had many imitators[1].

The *Life of Antony* accordingly assumes great importance as the record of a man who was an innovator, and the true founder of monasticism. We shall not appreciate monasticism properly until we realise that it was a new and startling development. "It came into existence at an ascertained point in the third century, and its novelty no doubt had much to do with the enthusiasm that greeted it[2]." The impression which it made on Augustine was almost overwhelming. "We listened with amazement to the tale of Thy Wonders, so freshly wrought, almost in our own life-time, so well attested, springing from the true faith and the bosom of the Catholic Church[3]."

Antony was born about 250, and was the son of a peasant proprietor of moderate means. Though brought up in comparative comfort, he remained illiterate and always refused to learn to read or write. When he was some twenty years old, his parents being now dead, he heard read in church the passage of the Gospel which contains our Lord's words to the rich ruler. Applying them to himself[4], he sold his land and distributed the proceeds, and then, after placing his sister in a house of virgins, devoted himself to the ascetic life. This he practised for fifteen years on the outskirts of his native village, taking counsel of other solitaries in the same district and giving himself up to prayer and labour[5]. He now began to realise the seriousness of his undertaking, and the fact that he had to strive with more than flesh and blood. A longing for solitude seized him, and he retired to the desert. After twenty years of this life, spent in prayer and conflicts with the powers of evil, the solitary was a solitary no longer. His abode was surrounded by seekers after God, who kept imploring him to come out and instruct them in the ascetic life. He complied, and began to organise Christian monachism,

---

[1] *Op. cit.* p. 12.  [2] E. W. Watson, *loc. cit.*

[3] *Conf.* VIII. 6 (Bigg's translation).

[4] As did Basil on a later occasion, see p. 24.

[5] *Vit. Ant.* 2, 3.

somewhere about the year 305[1]. Later on he retired to the
upper Thebaid into solitude once more, feeling that the press
of disciples was too great for his soul's health[2]. He is said
to have lived to be over a hundred years old and to have
died about 356.

There is no longer any necessity to discuss the authenticity
of Athanasius' *Life of Antony*, our main authority for the
career of the saint, since recent writers are unanimous in its
favour[3]. The following characteristics of the monastic ideal
as displayed in its pages may be noted[4]. (i) Asceticism is
cultivated, not for its own sake, but as a means to an end,
namely, the complete freeing of the soul, the purification
of the whole personality. (ii) "Enthusiasm" reappears in
the Church with the monks. By the side of the official
ministry is found a ministry of grace. (iii) Antony sets the
example, followed by so many ascetics in after years, of wide-
spread pastoral activities. "It was as if a physician had been
given by God to Egypt[5]." (iv) Miracles and revelations play
an important part. These are apt to deter the modern reader
and make him fail to appreciate the nobler side of the *Life*.
They must not however be neglected; it is a fact of deep
significance that these early monks were conscious of being
able to see and do supernatural things.

The type of monasticism that prevailed in Lower Egypt
at the time of Basil's visit may be conveniently termed
Antonian, though it is doubtful how far its characteristics
are due to Antony and how far they are of independent
growth. We have full descriptions of the life of the great
monasteries in the pages of Rufinus, Palladius, Sozomen,
Jerome and Cassian. Basil visited them when they were
at an earlier and less developed stage, but their main features

---

[1] προῆλθεν ὁ Ἀντώνιος ὥσπερ ἐκ τινός ἀδύτου μεμυσταγωγημένος καὶ θεοφορού-
μενος.  *Vit. Ant.* 14.

[2] *Vit. Ant.* 49.

[3] See especially Butler, *Lausiac History*, I. 215 ff. and Robertson, *Athanasius*,
pp. 188 ff. Some would suppose that Athanasius was only partially responsible
for its contents.

[4] Cf. Holl, *Enthusiasmus*, pp. 141—155, from which the following sentences
are in the main derived.

[5] *Vit. Ant.* 87.

must have been the same as those described by the later writers.

In Alexandria itself, or rather on the outskirts of the city[1], there were a number of monasteries, but the settlements at a distance from the haunts of men, such as Nitria and Scete in the desert south of Alexandria, enjoyed the greatest reputation. Amoun (Ammonius), a contemporary, but not apparently a disciple, of Antony[2], was the founder of Nitria, which at the time of Palladius' visit contained no fewer than 5000 monks. In later times this monastery was famous for its attachment to Origen's doctrines, and the "Four Tall Brothers" came from Nitria. Many of these monks were of Alexandrian origin and distinctly superior in education to the native Coptic-speaking monks. We are told that guests of good education were given a book to read instead of being obliged to do their share of manual labour[3]. The monks of Scete considered Macarius the Egyptian their founder, so-called to mark his native Egyptian origin and distinguish him from Macarius the Alexandrian[4].

Antony had been a solitary who collected disciples around him in spite of himself. But in "Antonian" monasticism the purely eremitic life tended to die out and be replaced by the semi-eremitic. There was generally a central church to which the occupants of the cells resorted on Saturdays and Sundays. Various trades were carried on, to preserve the ascetics from idleness and provide the scanty necessaries of life. There was little organisation and no fixed rule of life. "The elders exercised an authority; but it was mainly personal, and was but a supremacy of greater spiritual wisdom. The society appears to have been a sort of spiritual democracy, ruled by the personal influence of the leading ascetics....A young man would put himself under the guidance of a senior and obey

---

[1] Palladius spent three years in the monasteries round Alexandria, which contained some 2000 monks (*Hist. Laus.* VII. 1. Lucot's edition, 1912; subsequent references to Palladius will be made to this cheap and scholarly edition).

[2] Cf. *Vit. Ant.* 60.

[3] *Hist. Laus.* VII. 4; cf. XIII. 1 (ἄσκησις γραφική) and the account of Piterus in Socr. *HE.* IV. 23.

[4] *Hist. Laus.* XVII. 1.

him in all things; but the bonds between them were wholly
voluntary[1]." If the obedience to authority was voluntary, so
also was the amount of asceticism practised. But the public
opinion of the monastery demanded that it should be considerable, and the monks vied with one another in their feats of
physical endurance. Their spirit was quite that of the modern
athlete, and in fact "athlete" was an actual term used to
describe a distinguished monk[2].

As these monasteries were so near Alexandria, where Basil
stopped some little while, it is highly probable that he paid
them a visit, but there is no sign that they influenced him
in any way. On the other hand, he derived many features
of his system from the monks of the Pachomian obedience,
and so it is necessary to treat the other type of Egyptian
monachism in more detail[3].

Pachomius[4] was born about 290 in the neighbourhood of
Thebes, and came of heathen parents. After a brief period
of soldiering the charitable behaviour of the Christians at
Esneh attracted him to Christianity, and he spent some time
in a ruined temple of Serapis, leading an eremitic life in
common with a number of others[5]. This was near Schenesit
and he was about twenty years old at the time. The Christians
of the district recognised his piety, and presently he sought
the grace of baptism. Attracted by the fame of a hermit
named Palaemon he left his associates and sought the master's
cell. A number of ascetics were already under Palaemon's

---

[1] Butler, *Lausiac History*, I. 234.     [2] As it had been used of the Martyrs.

[3] Basil visited, besides Alexandria, "the rest of Egypt." The analogies
between Basilian and Pachomian institutions are close enough to necessitate a
personal visit to Tabennisi and its neighbours on Basil's part. At a later date
visitors such as Jerome could get their idea of cenobitism from the Pachomian
monastery at Canopus, but this apparently did not exist so early as 358.

[4] The best book is Ladeuze, *Étude sur le cénobitisme pakhomien* (Louvain,
1898). It is unfortunately out of print, and I have not been able to see a copy.
I rely for my knowledge of it on citations in later books and especially on the full
abstract given by Leclercq in his article "Cénobitisme" (*Dict. d'arch. chrét.*).
See also Amélineau, *Étude historique sur saint Pakhome*; Zöckler, *Askese und
Mönchtum*, pp. 192—211; Butler, *Lausiac History*, I. 155—158, 234—237. The
following account of Pachomius' life is drawn from Amélineau, and that of the
rules and institutions of his monasteries from Ladeuze (indirectly) and Zöckler.

[5] The supposition that he was a priest or devotee of Serapis is groundless.

direction; the discipline was very severe, long fasts and depri-
vation of sleep being practised, and the prescribed number
of prayers reaching the total of sixty by day and fifty by
night. The austerities were practised individually, and there
was no common life. After some years spent in this manner
Pachomius was called by an angelic vision to found a community of his own and legislate for the young monks. Retiring to Tabennisi, near Denderah on the Nile, he lived at
first by himself in a cell, but the advent of disciples made
it necessary to organise a proper monastery and draw up
a code of rules. As we shall see presently, his legislation
was remarkably original and bears the impress of a master-
mind. There was a natural tendency for the anchorites to
draw more closely together, but this in itself would not have
produced cenobitism, the credit of which must be ascribed to
Pachomius. It is not surprising that so epoch-making a
development was ascribed to divine intervention and the Rule
believed to have been brought by an angel. Pachomius died
about 346, by which time there were ten monasteries in all
under his rule, nine of men and one of women, and the total
number of ascetics reached 3000.

The Rule of Pachomius has come down to us in several
different versions and recensions. While it is impossible to
recover with certainty the first form of the Rule, the version
given by Palladius is marked by such primitive simplicity that
it cannot be far removed from the original[1].

The Rule is very short and does not attempt to cover the
ground. It was only intended for the weaker brethren, the
stronger not being thought to need a rule. It is chiefly concerned with prayer, meals and clothing. Prayers are to be
said to the extent of twelve during the day, twelve at twilight,
twelve at night, three at the ninth hour, with a psalm at each
meal. Communion is ordered for Saturday and Sunday. The
monks are to eat their meals all together in one place. The
amount of food is to be proportioned to the needs of the
individual, no hindrance being offered to his eating or fasting

---

[1] See *Hist. Laus.* XXXII. Ladeuze, *op. cit.* p. 272, says Jerome's version is
the best and Palladius has less authority.

as he pleases; but the more he eats, the more work must he do. Clothing is to consist of a *Lebiton*, a sleeveless linen under-garment, a *Melotes*, a garment made of white sheep-skin, a girdle, and a *Cucullium* or hood. The monks are to sleep three in a cell, in a sitting, not recumbent, position. A three years' probation, during which the postulant under-goes most laborious tasks, is ordered before admission to the community. Monks from other convents with a different rule are not to be admitted, though strangers may be entertained. The brethren are to be divided into twenty-four sections (τάγματα), called by the names of the twenty-four letters of the alphabet. The abbot in addressing the monks is to use the letter of their section, and the letters are meant to corre-spond with the characters of the monks in a mystical manner only intelligible to the initiated[1]. Such is the substance of the Rule which the angel is said to have brought. " Its clear-cut style, its quick advance from point to point, its freedom from casuistic detail, make us recognise its originality[2]."

However this is but a scanty description of the life of these important monasteries, and in order to compare them with Basil's institutions a fuller account must be given. It will be remembered that certain features of the later accounts may not have been developed at the time of Basil's visit in 358. Palladius, for example, did not come to Egypt till 388. But the close correspondence of Basil's Rules with the Pacho-mian system goes to show that the life of the Tabennisian monasteries at the earlier date was identical in all essentials with that depicted in the later documents. In any case the later developments of the Pachomian ideal at the hands of Schnoudi may be neglected as outside our range[3]. In giving a description of the monasteries it will be convenient to arrange

[1] Zöckler, *Askese und Mönchtum*, p. 207, compares the 24 sections into which at a later date the Akoimetai were divided for liturgical purposes. Ladeuze, p. 264, doubts this classification. Cf. however Butler, *Lausiac History*, II. 206.
[2] Zöckler, p. 203.
[3] Cf. Butler, *Lausiac History*, I. 236. "The aim of Bgoul and Schnoudi in their great monastery at Athribis was to combine with the cenobitical life the austerities of Nitria." Schnoudi made his monks take a formal *vow* of obedience, which was not exacted at Tabennisi. See Leipoldt, *Schenute von Atripe*.

the material under the same heads as those which we shall use
for analysing the Basilian Rules in Chapter VI.

I. *Joining the monastery.*

(*a*) *Renunciation of possessions.*

The monk had no further need of his possessions, which
he ceded to the monastery[1].

(*b*) *Admission to the community.*

None were refused unless they had led bad lives hitherto,
and were such as would require constant watching. Slaves
were not accepted because they had not control over their own
persons. No formal vows existed in the original Pachomian
monasteries[2].

II. *Life in the monastery.*

(*a*) *Prayer.*

Frequent prayers were insisted on, but it is not quite
clear what were the exact hours of prayer. Punctuality
was enforced. The whole body of monks assembled in
church only for the greater services, probably four times
a day[3].

(*b*) *Meals.*

There were two meals a day; flesh and wine were forbidden, but otherwise no special abstinence was enjoined.
The mid-day meal was taken in sections, in order that work
might be interrupted as little as possible. The general
community fasts were twice a week. Special food was
allowed for invalids[4].

---

[1] Leclercq (summarising Ladeuze), col. 3117; cf. Basil, B. 85, 92, 304, 305.
(In the notes throughout the book Basil's *Regulae fusius tractatae* will for brevity
be denoted by F., and the *Regulae brevius tractatae* by B.). References to Basil's
Rules will only be given when the resemblances are more or less close. For the
precepts of the angelic "Rule," which are not repeated here, see above.

[2] Leclercq, 3115, 3116; Basil, F. 10, 11.

[3] See Butler, *Lausiac History*, II. 208.

[4] Leclercq, 3122 (but Ladeuze, pp. 58, 298, doubts this movable meal);
Zöckler, pp. 203, 204; Basil, F. 19, 21.

*(c)  Clothing.*

The new-comer quitted his secular clothes and assumed the religious habit[1].

*(d)  Work.*

Mat-making and basket-making ranked with agriculture as the most important trades. Work was done under the direction of a foreman, and another officer, the steward, was responsible for the sale of products. A monk had no claim to anything that he had made. Intellectual labour was also demanded. The illiterate had to learn to read, and the study of Scripture was compulsory[2].

III.  *Order and discipline.*

*The officers.*

The Superior had great authority; he could nominate the heads of the daughter monasteries, and Pachomius designated his successor. Twice every year, at Easter and on August 13th, a general chapter of the whole community was held. Under the Superior all were equal; all had to render unquestioning obedience to the Superior, or his deputy. Within the community monks could be transferred from one monastery to another at the discretion of the authorities[3].

IV.  *Various other points.*

*(a)  Earthly relationships.*

It was not permitted to see relations without the consent of the Superior and the presence of other brethren[4].

*(b)  Journeys.*

These were forbidden at first, but the rule was afterwards relaxed. As the community developed, they became necessary in order to sell produce. A deputation was sent to Alexandria from time to time[5].

---

[1] Leclercq, 3116; Basil, F. 22, B. 90. See above, p. 36.

[2] Leclercq, 3117, 3120, 3121; Basil, F. 38, B. 96, 141, 142, 235.

[3] Leclercq, 3097, 3117, 3118; Basil, F. 28, 49, B. 112. There were however stewards and other officers including a second-in-command (ὁ δευτερεύων, *Hist. Laus.* XXXII. 8); cf. Basil, F. 45.

[4] Leclercq, 3117; Basil, F. 32.      [5] Leclercq, 3120, 3122; Basil, F. 44.

### V. *Relations with outside world.*

### (a) *The official Church.*

Pachomius was at first viewed with suspicion by the Church authorities and was condemned at a synod of bishops. However, he showed great deference to the bishops both in doctrine and practical matters, and the visit of Athanasius in 330 set the seal of official approval on his work[1].

### (b) *Neighbouring monasteries.*

Considerable opposition was experienced from the non-Pachomian monks. This is not surprising in view of the innovations that Pachomius introduced into the ascetic life as hitherto understood. It was not until the rule of his successor Orsisius that friendly relations were established with Antony; till then the two branches of monasticism had no connexion with one another[2].

### (c) *Convents of women.*

About the same time that Pachomius settled at Tabennisi, his sister Mary went to the opposite bank of the Nile and began to gather disciples around her. This soon became a proper nunnery; it was completely under the control of the Superior of the monks, who delegated elderly men to care for its discipline. Within a few years of Pachomius' death two other sisterhoods were formed. Elaborate precautions were taken to prevent the monks and nuns from meeting. When a nun died, her companions brought her body to the river bank and then retired; presently the monks fetched away the corpse in a boat and carried out the funeral ceremonies[3].

The general lines of Pachomian monachism are clearly defined, alike in earlier and later accounts. The community

[1] Leclercq, 3096; Zöckler, p. 199.  [2] Leclercq, 3097; Zöckler, p. 200.

[3] Leclercq, 3095, 3118; Zöckler, p. 208. We are reminded of Basil's monastery on one side of the Iris and Macrina's on the other. Palladius gives an interesting account of the nunneries. The men and women were economically inter-dependent, the men providing food and doing rough work for the women (*Hist. Laus.* XXXII. 9, XXXIII. 2), while the women made clothes for the men. (See Ladeuze, p. 303). Clerical monks went to celebrate the Communion, apparently on Sunday only (XXXIII. 2). The "presbyter" was responsible for discipline (XXXIII. 4, cf. XXXIV. 4). See pp. 104, 105.

was a model of skilful organisation. The great numbers
of the monks necessitated an iron discipline and a military
rather than family system. Work and prayer were the two
master ideas of Pachomius, though no doubt in the eyes of
some contemporaries work would have appeared to predomi-
nate unduly, and the true spirit of asceticism to evaporate.
The austerities prescribed seem burdensome to a European,
but they were conceived in a spirit of moderation. " The
fundamental idea of St Pachomius' rule was to establish
a moderate level of observance which might be obligatory
upon all ; and then to leave it open to each—and to indeed
encourage each—to go beyond the fixed minimum, according
as he was prompted by his strength, his courage and his
skill[1]." Such is Dom Butler's summing up, and he points
out that even in Pachomius the spirit of Egyptian monachism
remains strongly individualistic, and alien to the true ideal of
the common life. Certainly there is no proof that Pachomius
considered community life the higher form of monachism or
disputed the right of the individual to live by himself if he
could. Much as Basil derived from Pachomius, his eloquent
vindication of the superiority of the common life was not a
product of his Egyptian visit[2].

After his visit to Egypt, Basil proceeded to Palestine,
Coele-Syria and Mesopotamia[3]. He had come to Egypt by
way of Syria without, apparently, making any lengthy stop
on the way[4]. On his return journey he went to Palestine,
perhaps making a short stay at Jerusalem[5]; then northwards
to Syria, and finally to Mesopotamia. Edessa, in the north-
west angle of Mesopotamia, is as far as we need imagine him

---

[1] Butler, *Lausiac History*, I. 236.
[2] See p. 85. Egypt was of course full of monks. The two most characteristic systems have been discussed, but there were many varieties of ascetic life of
an unorganised type.
[3] *Ep.* 223.                     [4] *ib.* I.
[5] In *Ep.* 45 Basil writes to a lapsed monk with whom he had once lived at
Jerusalem. As Basil cannot have stayed more than a few weeks in that city,
Maran considers the letter spurious. Jackson suggests that we should take
Jerusalem "in a figurative sense for the companionship of the saints." This is
possible, but the letter does not imply a prolonged stay. But the authenticity of
the letter is doubtful on other grounds, see pp. 108, 111.

to have gone[1]. The natural route home would be by Samosata and Melitene. Owing to the mountains that intervened
between the Euphrates and Cappadocia the last part of the
journey must have been completed in the summer months,
probably those of 358[2]. It is interesting to think of Basil,
after seeing the Coptic-speaking monks, visiting Edessa, the
historic centre of the Syriac-speaking Church. Ephraem the
Syrian did not make his home at Edessa until after the fall
of Nisibis in 363, so Basil and he can hardly have met. If
however, as seems likely, Basil passed through Samosata, the
foundations of his friendship with Eusebius of Samosata may
have been laid on this occasion[3].

The state of monasticism in these lands at the time of
Basil's visit need not detain us long; there is no sign that he
was in any way influenced by what he saw, unless perhaps by
way of reaction. The monastic life had been introduced into
Palestine early in the fourth century by Hilarion, one of
Antony's disciples. The original impulse to the eremitic life
survived, and the cenobitic ideal made little headway in
Palestine either now or later. In Syria and Mesopotamia
asceticism was, so to speak, indigenous. Whether or not
influences from the Far East are to be postulated, it is clear
that Christianity had from an early date assumed a distinc-
tively ascetic form. There existed certain "Sons of the
Covenant," about whom much discussion has arisen. They
were celibates and practised asceticism in other ways, but
were not exactly monks. Professor Burkitt has maintained
that they were simply the baptised laity of the Syriac Church,
who were bound to a life of continence and freedom from

---

[1] The time at our disposal—about a year—compels us to cut down his travels
as far as possible. The available time is shortened by his illness at Alexandria.

[2] In *Ep.* 1 Basil writes from Alexandria and refers to his ailments. Unless
he recovers, he will be unable to meet his correspondent, even in the coming
winter. But this throws little light on the chronology for (1) we do not know
where he expected to meet his correspondent, (2) the letter is highly rhetorical.
Ramsay refers to the cessation of travel during the winter (Hastings' *D.B.* v.
377; cf. Bas. *Epp.* 20, 27, 191, 198). But he is not justified in taking Basil as
"a fair specimen of ancient views," as his health was notoriously frail.

[3] We learn of Eusebius as bishop of Samosata first in 361.

worldly cares[1]. In any case the seeds of monasticism found congenial soil in these districts and a luxuriant crop resulted. Mar Awgin (Eugenius) is said to have introduced cenobitism into Mesopotamia, after a sojourn in Pachomius' monastery. During the fourth century monks after the Egyptian pattern existed by the side of ascetics like Aphraates, who has been termed *un moine de l'ancien régime*[2]. But the eremitic type predominated ; cenobitism was valued only as a preparation for the higher solitary life. The most extravagant mortifications were practised, and an element of the Indian Fakir was undoubtedly present. To the Syrian monks must be ascribed a considerable part of the discredit which has attached to the idea of asceticism in modern times[3].

[1] *Early Eastern Christianity*, pp. 125—142 ; cf. Connolly's criticisms in *Journ. Theo. Stud.* July, 1905.

[2] Leclercq, *op. cit.* col. 3140.

[3] Cf. Soz. *HE.* VI. 32—34; Theodoret, *HE.* IV. 23—25 and *Hist. Rel.*

# CHAPTER IV

## ST BASIL AS MONK AND BISHOP

AFTER a year or more spent in visiting the monasteries of the East, Basil could claim a first-hand acquaintance with the methods of the greatest exponents of asceticism. He had returned home full of admiration for what he had seen. But it was hardly to be expected that a man of aristocratic family, fresh from a brilliant University career, and conversant with the ideals of European civilisation and culture, should wish to set up in his native land an exact reproduction of the life led by Egyptian peasants. Basil had both genius and originality, and he was responsible for important changes in the theory and practice of monasticism as hitherto understood. In order to appreciate these changes we must now study Basil's life from the ascetic point of view. The present chapter will first re-tell the famous story of the retreat in Pontus, and then describe Basil's later activities in the monastic field, especially during his episcopate; the other sides of his life will only be mentioned incidentally. The two following chapters will be devoted to an examination of the ascetic writings attributed to Basil and a discussion of their contents. This method will entail a certain amount of repetition, and in some respects is inferior to the alternative plan of making a composite picture from all the available data. But since the genuineness of the *Ascetica* has been frequently disputed, the method adopted seems the only scientific way of treating the subject.

With the help of Basil's own letters and the writings of the two Gregories it is possible to get a clearly-defined picture of the early life in Pontus; but in later years the importance of the doctrinal controversies in which Basil was involved over-shadows the ascetic side of his life, both in his own writings and those of his contemporaries.  In consequence our informa-tion with respect to the later period is meagre, and interesting problems must often be left unsolved.  Basil's letters, where available, are by far the best authority.  The orations of the two Gregories contain some genuine history, but are rhetorical and laudatory in the highest degree[1].

In the summer of 358, so it seems, Basil returned to Caesarea.  Some writers have assigned his return to the previous year, in order presumably to allow more time for the first stay in Pontus, which was abruptly closed by the summons to the Council of Constantinople (360).  But this only makes it very difficult to fit in the events that occurred before his travels in the East.  The years 356—360 must have been in any case very crowded, and the restless energy of Basil's spirit enabled him to defy his physical frailty and accomplish a great deal in a brief space of time.

Basil now resolved to embrace a life of asceticism, and called upon Gregory to join him and thus fulfil a promise made in student days at Athens.  Tiberina was suggested as a possible locality; its vicinity to Gregory's home recom-mended it to the latter, and for a time perhaps Basil thought seriously of the proposal.  But the charm of a spot in Pontus near Annesi, the home of his boyhood, led him to propose it as an alternative.  The two friends had a lively passage of arms over the merits of the rival places, and taunting refer-ences were made to the mud of Tiberina and the Cimmerian darkness of Pontus.  This part of the correspondence was written in jest and need not be taken seriously.  Gregory however had some cause to be annoyed with his friend.  He had pointed out that he could not desert his parents com-pletely, and had made the perfectly fair proposal that they should live together, spending half of the time near his home and the other half where Basil chose.  Basil rejected Tiberina

---

[1] Boulenger in his *Grégoire de Nazianze, Discours funèbres*, pp. xxix—xxxii, shows how the whole structure of *Or.* 43 is modelled on the existing rules of rhetoric.

and chose a spot in the neighbourhood of his own home, and then expected Gregory to acquiesce in his decision. Gregory was somewhat offended, and refused on this occasion to pay more than a brief visit to his imperious friend[1].

About this time must be placed Basil's renunciation of his possessions. It could not have been before his travels, which must have cost a considerable sum of money. The words of Gregory and his own letters prove that Basil did make a definite act of renunciation[2]. But he cannot have given all away. His brother betrays this when he describes Basil as "the man who ungrudgingly spent upon the poor his patrimony even before he was a priest, and most of all in the time of the famine...and afterwards did not hoard even what remained to him[3]." Maran explains Gregory's words by supposing that about the time of the famine Basil came in for some property by the death of his mother Emmelia[4]. But the passage as a whole gives a different impression, and so do certain allusions in Basil's writings. He probably sold his personal possessions and gave the proceeds to the poor; but to dispose of his share in the family property was less easy. It seems likely that he dedicated to God his income from this source and spent it as occasion required. This conclusion is supported by the somewhat ambiguous answers given by Basil in the Rules on the subject of worldly possessions[5].

Basil's personality has impressed itself so deeply on later monasticism that we naturally think of him as the pioneer of the movement in Asia Minor. Strictly speaking, this was not the case. Communications between the different parts of the Empire were frequent and easy, and the great ascetic movement in Egypt and Syria must have had echoes beyond the Taurus before Basil retired to Pontus. Just as Antony found

---

[1] Greg. Naz. *Epp.* 1, 2, 4, 5, 6; Bas. *Ep.* 14.
[2] Greg. Naz. *Or.* 43, 60; Bas. *Ep.* 223.
[3] Greg. Nyss. *In Eunom.* 1. 10.     [4] *Vit. Bas.* IV. 2.
[5] See pp. 81—83. Cf. *Ep.* 3, where he complains of an attack made on his property, which disturbs his tranquillity; also *Ep.* 37, from which we learn that Basil retained certain rights in a property made over to his foster-parents by his parents. For a later tradition cf. Cassian, *Inst.* VII. 19.

ascetics on the outskirts of his village ready to instruct him[1], so it was here.　No sooner do the lives of the great Cappadocians light up the prevailing darkness than we discern in the background a multitude of persons already pledged to the ascetic life.　Gregory of Nazianzus relates how he hesitated which of the two methods of asceticism to choose, whether to be a solitary, or to live a celibate life in the world, devoted to prayer and active benevolence[2].　These two modes of asceticism were therefore already well known.　Basil's great contribution to Church life consisted in the fact that, as Gregory tells us, he instituted a middle way between the two extremes, combining the excellences of both[3].　The presence of such ascetics is presupposed in the story of Basil's life, for disciples came to him in large numbers as soon as he settled in Pontus.　The ascetic life was there already; Basil's task was to organise it, and provide it with institutions suited to the needs of the country and people.　And further, the great army of ascetics, both male and female, to whom we find references in Basil's letters, cannot all have owed their inspiration to his teaching and example.　Time will not admit of so rapid a development.　We know the name of one of these precursors of Basil, the famous Eustathius of Sebaste, about whom a few words must now be said[4].

We have already seen that Eustathius' advice may have led Basil to visit Egypt and Syria[5].　In any case he came under the influence of the bishop of Sebaste on his return. "So when I beheld certain men in my own country striving to copy their ways, I felt that I had found a help to my own salvation....Though many were for withdrawing me from their society, I would not allow it, because I saw that they put a life of endurance before a life of pleasure ; and, because

---

[1] See p. 30.

[2] *Carm.* XI. 300 ff. ; cf. I. 65 ff.　He calls the two classes ἄζυγοι and μιγάδες. The above interpretation seems the most probable.　See Additional Note B.

[3] *Or.* 43, 62.

[4] See Appendix A for a discussion of the significance of Eustathius.

[5] p. 24.　Possibly he had known and admired Eustathius at an even earlier date.　In *Ep.* 244 he writes: "You have been, as it were, amazed and astounded, at the idea of the change in the notorious Basil.　Why, ever since he was a boy he did such and such service to such a one (*i.e.* Eustathius)."

of the extraordinary excellence of their lives, I became an eager supporter of them[1]." Sozomen tells us that Eustathius "founded a society of monks in Armenia, Paphlagonia and Pontus, and became the author of a zealous discipline," and elsewhere describes him as "a leader of the best monks[2]." It seems then that Eustathius had already founded monasteries in Pontus, and that Basil received at his hands the last and most fruitful of the lessons he took in asceticism. Friendly relations continued, and Eustathius was a frequent visitor at Annesi. "How often," asks Basil, "did you visit me in my monastery on the Iris?...How many days did we spend in the opposite village, at my mother's, living as friend with friend, and discoursing together night and day[3]?" Into the subsequent breach of the friendship and Basil's recriminations we need not enter. There must have been two sides to the question, and Eustathius' case has to go by default. It is quite certain that Basil owed much to his early teacher. In spite of personal and doctrinal disagreements he never finds fault with his asceticism. It has been supposed by some that Basil's *cenobitic* institutions at least were his own, but even of this we cannot be certain. If the Basilian Rules could be ascribed to Eustathius without manifest absurdity, it seems probable that their ideas were to a large extent those of the bishop of Sebaste[4].

The spot which had so commended itself to Basil by its natural beauty and adaptability to monastic purposes was on the banks of the Iris; Annesi, where his mother and sister were living, was on the opposite bank of the river. The

[1] *Ep.* 223.    [2] *HE.* III. 14, VIII. 27.
[3] *Ep.* 223.
[4] See Sozomen, *HE.* III. 14. It is significant that Basil calls Eustathius' monastery "the brotherhood" (*Ep.* 223), the special word he uses of his own foundations. On the whole subject see Loofs, *Eustathius von Sebaste*. Maran (*Vit. Bas.* VI. 2) considers that the disciples of Eustathius were monks living two or three together, *i.e.* "Sarabaites," such as abbot Piamun found in large numbers in Pontus and Armenia (Cassian, *Coll.* XVIII. 7). Sozomen (*HE.* VI. 34) says that the severity of the climate prevented the solitary life. It is clear that here, as in Egypt, another form of monachism existed by the side of the cenobitic. There is however no reason to ascribe it to Eustathius. On the contrary, the fact that Basil was originally Eustathius' disciple and never apparently broke away from his ascetic ideals, points to an opposite conclusion.

district was close to Neo-Caesarea, but was under the ecclesiastical jurisdiction of Ibora[1].  The description, says Sir W. M.
Ramsay, " can hardly refer to any other part of the river than
the rocky glen below Turkhal[2]."  This is marked in modern
maps some 30 miles S.E. of Amasia.  Basil's glowing words
have been often quoted.  " There is a lofty mountain covered
with thick woods, watered toward the north with cool and
transparent streams.  A plain lies beneath, enriched by the
waters which are ever draining off from it ; and skirted by
a spontaneous profusion of trees almost thick enough to be a
fence ; so as even to surpass Calypso's island, which Homer
seems to have considered the most beautiful spot on the earth.
Indeed it is like an island, enclosed as it is on all sides ; for
deep hollows cut off two sides of it ; the river, which has
lately fallen down a precipice, runs all along the front, and is
impassable as a wall ; while the mountain extending itself
behind, and meeting the hollows in a crescent, stops up the
path at its roots.  There is but one pass, and I am master of
it.  Behind my abode there is another gorge, rising into a
ledge above, so as to command the extent of the plains and
the stream which bounds it, which is not less beautiful, to my
taste, than the Strymon as seen from Amphipolis....Shooting
down from the rocks, and eddying in a deep pool, it (the
stream) forms a most pleasant scene for myself or anyone
else : and is an inexhaustible source to the country people,
in the countless fish which its depths contain.  What need
to tell of the exhalations from the earth, or the breezes
from the river ?  Another might admire the multitude of
flowers, and singing birds ; but leisure I have none for such
thoughts[3]."

Such was Basil's description of the place to his friend
Gregory, who seems to have paid a brief visit, and then to
have left, only to find the attraction of a monastic life with

---

[1] Greg. Nyss. *In XL Mart.* (*P.G.* XLVI. 784.)

[2] *Hist. Geog. of Asia Minor*, p. 326.  The name is variously spelt in the
maps.

[3] *Ep.* 14.  I have not seen the suggestion made, but was not this part of
the family estate?

Basil irresistible and return for a more permanent stay[1]. Perhaps Basil thought of the place in fine weather, while Gregory remembered cold and wet days, for, half in jest, half in earnest, he gives quite a different account. The place was shut in by mountains, so that the sun was rarely seen. The ground was encumbered by thorn-bushes, and was too precipitous for safe walking. The roar of the river drowned the voice of psalmody. He shuddered at the recollection of the biting winds, the cheerlessness of their hut, their fruitless labours in the so-called garden, and the poverty of their meals. Their teeth could make no impression on the solid hunks of bread, and speedy starvation would have been their fate had it not been for the opportune assistance of Basil's mother[2]. There is a good deal of humorous exaggeration in this, yet the hardships endured by Basil and his companions, especially during the first winter, that of 358—359, must have been considerable.

In his fifth letter Gregory alludes to the presence of Basil's mother, who lived on the opposite bank of the river. Yielding to her daughter's entreaties, Emmelia had renounced the world in company with Macrina and Peter, as soon as the business affairs of the family were sufficiently settled to make such a course possible[3]. A short account of the later years of Basil's mother and sister will not be out of place here. Our chief authority is the beautiful *Life of Macrina*, of which Dr Harnack says: "We obtain perhaps the clearest and truest impression of the piety of the Greek Church from reading the biography of sister Macrina, by Gregory of Nyssa[4]."

About the time of Basil's return from Athens, but before

[1] The editors of Gregory in the *Nicene and Post-Nicene Fathers* assign letters 4—6, written obviously about the same time, to the year 361. But Basil's fourteenth letter, to which Gregory's fourth is an answer, belongs to c. 358, at the beginning of the Pontic retreat. These letters must therefore be transferred to 358 or 359, in which case Gregory's testimony in 6 becomes important. The cenobium was properly organised from the first, with "written Rules and Canons."

[2] Greg. Naz. *Epp.* 4—6.     [3] See p. 23.

[4] *History of Dogma*, III. 180. I cannot see the justice of Schäfer's remark: "Freilich ist schon vieles stark idealisiert und ins Wunderbare gezogen, so dass man bei der Verwendung vorsichtig sein muss." *Basilius des Grossen Beziehungen zum Abendlande*, p. 11.

the death of Naucratius, Macrina persuaded her mother to give up the comforts and privileges of her rank, and live a life similar to that of her serving-women. After the tragic end of Naucratius, Macrina was able to lead her mother to a further stage of virtue. Most of the family property was by this time divided among the children, so that the step towards a more rigid asceticism was easy to take. Class distinctions were now so far obliterated in the household that the two ladies shared one table with the maidservants and slept in the same kind of bed. It was an ideal life; no pride or disputing marred the harmony; prayer and psalmody went on without interruption. The household of women had the enthusiastic support of Peter, the youngest child, who had been brought up entirely by Macrina. He lived with them and helped them in every way, "coöperating with them in their efforts after the angelic life[1]." The periodical visits of Basil must also have been a great encouragement and inspiration. The picture is one of rare beauty. We look in vain for any parallel to this life of devotion, shared by men and women, master and servant, until we come to Nicholas Ferrar's household at Little Gidding in the seventeenth century. The combination of earnest asceticism with the life of a well-ordered household, and simple and natural relations between the sexes, is as unusual as it is pleasing.

When Emmelia died in the arms of her children, Basil had become bishop of Caesarea. The household, to which women had been drawn as disciples for some time past, seems now to have become more definitely a monastery. Gregory describes his visit to his sister in her last illness. The nuns had a church of their own, in which they were chanting vespers at the time of his arrival, and Macrina bade him join them. After her death he consulted with Vestiana, a nun of noble birth, about the funeral arrangements. Macrina had given instructions that nothing but the commonest materials should be used. In preparing her body for the funeral, Vestiana found that she had worn an iron cross and a ring of the same material next to her skin. She bade Gregory

[1] *Vit. Macr.* (*P. G.* XLVI. 965—972).

and the nuns come and observe these marks of Macrina's sanctity. Anyone who is familiar with fourth century literature will realise how unpleasant this incident might have been made in the hands of Christian writers; but Gregory treats it with simplicity and delicacy. The funeral drew a vast crowd of mourners, and Araxius, the local bishop, gave the address[1]. As Basil is revered in the Eastern Church as the traditional father of the monastic life for men, so Macrina ranks as the founder of women's convent life. There are few women in Church History whose influence, direct and indirect, has been so great, or who have so well deserved the title of "Saint."

Let us now re-cross the river and return to Basil. It is clear that he began his monastery on a definite system from the outset. With Gregory's help on his first visit he sketched rules for the cenobium, and began the round of prayer, labour and study. Building, agriculture, the study of Scripture, vigils, prayers and psalmody are all referred to in Gregory's letter recalling this visit[2]. We need not ask where the brethren came from. The impulse to an ascetic life had already been given, and when a man like Basil, who possessed personal as well as family prestige, joined the movement, he was bound to attract followers. By the end of 359 things were in such good order that Basil could leave his work to attend the Council of Constantinople in 360.

The length of Basil's stay in Pontus has been exaggerated. Rufinus records a tradition that Basil and Gregory spent thirteen years in retirement[3]. If we could assume that all the time between 358 and 370, the date of Basil's elevation to the episcopate, was spent in Pontus, the reckoning would be approximately correct; but as a matter of fact he was only there for a small portion of the time. In 360 he went to Constantinople, after which he returned to Caesarea. In 361 we find him at Nazianzus in company with Gregory. In 362 he

---

[1] *Vit. Macr.* 972—993. For Basil's regulations for nuns see pp. 104, 105.
[2] Greg. Naz. *Ep.* 6.
[3] It is no more than a tradition. "Ibique per annos (ut aiunt) tredecim, omnibus Graecorum saecularium libris remotis, solis divinae Scripturae voluminibus operam dabant." Ruf. *H.E.* II. 9.

was present at the deathbed of Dianius, bishop of Caesarea[1]. Basil seems also to have had a good deal to do with the election of Eusebius as Dianius' successor and was himself ordained priest about this time[2]. The prominent position taken by Basil in the Church of the metropolis roused the jealousy of Eusebius; the monks of Caesarea championed Basil and there was some danger of a schism. "Whereupon," says Gregory, "with my advice and earnest encouragement on the point, he set out from the place with me into Pontus, and presided over the abodes of contemplation (i.e. monasteries) there. He himself too founded one worthy of mention[3]." This was towards the end of 362 or at the beginning of 363. In 365 the trouble that threatened the Church of Caesarea through the approach of Valens drew Basil back to the post of danger[4]. The task of directing the practical activities of the Church occupied the remaining years of his life. He cannot then have spent more than three or four years in Pontus, while Gregory's time was even less[5].

Basil's life in Pontus may therefore be divided into two parts, the first lasting a little over a year (358—359) and ending with his departure to Constantinople, the second part (362—365) beginning with his flight from Caesarea to avoid a strife with Eusebius and ending with his return at the time of Valens' visit. Such a division does not exclude the possibility of several short visits between 360 and 362, and after 365[6]. It

---

[1] Bas. *Ep.* 51.

[2] Maran and others put his ordination in 364, but the view has not found many supporters. See Schäfer, *Basilius des Grossen Beziehungen zum Abendlande*, p. 50, for the reasons that support the date 362.

[3] Greg. Naz. *Or.* 43, 29. Cf. Soz. *H.E.* VI. 15. According to Gregory a number of monasteries already existed. Basil's monastery referred to must be the one he founded in 358.

[4] Greg. Naz. *Or.* 43, 30; Soz. *ib.*

[5] Pargoire's conclusion (*Dict. d'Archéol. chrét.* art. "Basile") would seem an over-estimate. "Ainsi Basile ne séjourna guère en tout que cinq ou six ans dans sa fondation d'Annesi." Morison, *St Basil and his Rule*, pp. xii, 7, allows three years for the stay in Pontus, 358—361, and overlooks the second visit.

[6] See Bas. *Ep.* 210, written from Annesi about 375. Looking back on his life he says: "Hither have I often retreated, and here have I spent many years, when endeavouring to escape from the hubbub of public affairs." Strictly speaking, parts of many years rather than many whole years were spent at Annesi after his childhood.

is reasonable to suppose that the first period, 358—359, was occupied with the organisation of his monastery at Annesi, and that his widespread propaganda, presently to be mentioned, fell within the second period.

Two among Basil's letters describe the life of the cenobia, the second, sent to Gregory in 358 or 359, and the twenty-second, *On the perfection of the life of solitaries*, addressed to an unknown destination at a later time. A summary of these must now be given, because the correspondence between the picture which they present and that which appears in the Basilian Rules is a strong argument for the authenticity of the latter. The second epistle has been justly described as a first sketch of the Rules.

There is only one way, says Basil in this letter, of escaping from the daily round of anxieties which weigh down the soul, and that is separation from the world—not only bodily separation, but severance of the soul from the world. This is the indispensable preliminary. For this purpose solitude, and such a retired place as we have here, are necessary[1]. We soothe the mind with exercises of piety, beginning the day with prayer and song, and then betake ourselves to our daily labour, seasoning it throughout with devotion[2]. "Thus the mind, saved from dissipation from without, and not through the senses thrown upon the world, falls back upon itself, and thereby ascends to the contemplation of God." The chief method of learning our duty is the study of Scripture, and the imitation of the examples contained therein[3]. "Prayers, too, after reading, find the soul fresher, and more vigorously stirred by love towards God." Restraint in conversation is of the utmost importance, and the cultivation of a "middle tone of voice." Outward appearance should be neglected and rough, to correspond with the inner humility of the soul. The one aim of dress is to give sufficient warmth; a girdle is to be worn[4], and bright colours or soft materials must be avoided. "The shoes should be cheap but serviceable[5]." As for food,

---

[1] See p. 81 ; cf. F. (*regulae fusius tractatae*) 6.
[2] pp. 86—88; F. 37.          [3] pp. 91, 95; B. (*brevius*) 235.
[4] p. 89; F. 23.              [5] p. 89; F. 22.

bread, water and vegetables will suffice, if a man is in good
health[1]. Grace should be said before and after eating. " Let
there be one fixed hour for taking food, always the same in
regular course, that of all the four and twenty hours of the
day and night barely this one may be spent upon the body[2]."
Sleep is to be light and purposely broken for meditation.
Especially at midnight is the ascetic's soul alone with God, and
wrapt in earnest prayer[3].

If this letter represents the ideals which animated Basil
in his early days at Annesi, the twenty-second letter shows
the cenobia at a more developed stage. Some monks have
asked his advice about doubtful points in the ascetic life. He
writes a brief tract in reply, in which he claims that his
injunctions are founded on a study of the inspired Scripture,
and announces his intention of leaving behind him definite
information in an easily intelligible form, for the benefit of
future students. Leaving out a number of precepts which
concern the life of all Christians rather than the special needs
of monks, to which, however, numerous parallels from the
Rules might be adduced, we notice the following points.

Silence is to be observed as far as possible. Strangers
who enter are not to speak to the brethren without the leave
of the overseers[4]. Wine and flesh meat must be eschewed[5].
Whatever "the Christian" possesses is given him to be used
and not hoarded up; he must take care of everything as the
Lord's property[6]. He must never murmur at scarcity of food
or excess of labour[7]; "the responsibility in these matters lies
with such as have authority in them." The voice should be
properly modulated and the eye under restraint. Ostentation
in clothing or food is forbidden. All must work, even those
engaged in more directly spiritual activities. " The Christian
ought not to change over from one work to another without
the approval of those who are appointed for the arrangement

---

[1] p. 89; F. 19, where however fish is allowed.
[2] p. 88; F. 21; B. 136. Apparently there was only one meal at first, and
Basil in the Rules modified this early austerity.
[3] p. 87; F. 37.                         [4] p. 90; B. 141.
[5] p. 89; F. 19.                         [6] p. 90; F. 41; B. 143, 144.
[7] pp. 89, 90; F. 18, 29; B. 71, 121, 131—134.

of such matters....Everyone ought to remain in his appointed post, not to go beyond his own bounds and intrude into what is not commanded him, unless the responsible authorities judge anyone to be in need of aid. No one ought to be found going from one workshop to another[1]." If a man offends, he is to be admonished, and if he then fails to amend himself, he must be brought before the Superior ($\tau\hat{\omega}$ $\pi\rho\sigma\epsilon\sigma\tau\hat{\omega}\tau\iota$). If he is obstinate, he is to be cut off, as a limb from the body[2]. Immoderate toil is to be avoided[3], just as much as unnecessary abundance of food or raiment.

The parallels between these two letters and the Rules are close, as will be seen from the footnotes. But if the Rules are compared with the earlier letter and the rest of the Basil-Gregory correspondence, it will be seen that they are conceived in a spirit of moderation, and that Basil did not recommend the average monk to imitate the privations of his own early monastic days[4]. In this respect he resembles Pachomius and Benedict, both of whom when legislating for disciples modified the severity of their original ideals.

Busy as Gregory and Basil must have been in their monastery with the claims of devotion and manual labour, they were nevertheless able to accomplish some important literary work. The compilation of choice passages from Origen, under the title of the *Philocalia*, was a product of their scanty leisure; it is still extant, and of great value to the student of Origen[5]. Besides this, the two friends drew up some rules for the monastic life[6].

Sozomen, Socrates and Rufinus give brief accounts of the

---

[1] p. 90; B. 117, 119, 142.

[2] p. 96; F. 28. ὁ προεστώς is the usual word in the Rules for the Superior, the various periphrases for the other officers are also characteristic, and are natural at an early stage of the institutions before a hierarchy of officials was established. See pp. 92 ff.

[3] B. 125.

[4] See Greg. Naz. *Or.* 43, 61; Greg. Nyss. *In laud. Bas.* In F. 19, 21 two meals a day are allowed and also a better quality of food. According to Boulenger (*Grégoire de Nazianze, Discours funèbres,* p civ) Gregory's description of Basil's dress and régime in *Or.* 43, 61 is borrowed from similar descriptions of Cynic-Stoic philosophers.

[5] Greg. Naz. *Ep.* 115. Gregory sent a copy in 382 to Theodore of Tyana.

[6] *ib.* 6.

work of Gregory and Basil outside their own monastery. Sozomen, who is a good authority for the monachism of Asia Minor, relates how they championed the Nicene doctrines and refuted Arianism. They divided the country between them "either by mutual agreement, or, as I have been informed, by lot. The cities in the neighbourhood of Pontus fell to Basil; and here he founded numerous monasteries, and, by teaching the people, he persuaded them to hold like views with himself[1]." Socrates gives a similar, if somewhat confused, version[2]. Rufinus tells us that they set out by different ways to the same task. Basil went through the cities and rural districts of Pontus, and stirred up the sluggish and indifferent minds of the inhabitants; he taught them to put away worldly things, to build monasteries, to find time for prayers and sacred music, to attend to the needs of the poor and provide them with proper houses and the necessaries of life, and to furnish recruits to the virgin life. " In a short space of time the face of the whole province was so changed, that it seemed as if an abundant crop and a joyful vineyard had sprung up in an arid and neglected countryside[3]." Probably Sozomen's account is the most accurate; he mentions Basil's work in the cities of Pontus, and is silent about the country districts. This agrees best with Basil's well-known policy of bringing the monasteries into connexion with the bishops and "village-bishops" ($\chi\omega\rho$-$\epsilon\pi\iota\sigma\kappa\sigma\pi\sigma\iota$)[4], and Cassian's testimony that Piamun found cenobia only in the towns of Pontus[5].

This activity for some reason or other aroused considerable opposition, especially among the citizens of Neo-Caesarea.

---

[1] *H.E.* VI. 17.    [2] *H.E.* IV. 26.

[3] Rufin. *H.E.* II. 9, "Verum cum iam ipsi sufficienter instructi divina dispensatione ad imbuendos populos vocarentur, et alius alio itinere, ad idem tamen opus uterque traheretur, Basilius Ponti urbes et rura circumiens, desides gentis illius animos et parum de spe futura sollicitos stimulare verbis, et praedicatione succendere, callumque ab his longae neglegentiae caepit abolere, subegitque, abiectis inanium rerum et saecularium curis, suimet notitiam recipere, in unum coire, monasteria construere, psalmis et hymnis et orationibus docuit vacare, pauperum curam gerere, eisque habitacula honesta, et quae ad victum necessaria sunt, praebere, virgines instituere, pudicam castamque vitam omnibus pene desiderabilem facere. Ita brevi permutata est totius provinciae facies, ut in arido et squalenti campo videretur seges foecunda, ac laeta vinea surrexisse."

[4] See p. 19.    [5] Cass. *Coll.* XVIII. 7.

We find the opposition reflected in a letter of Basil to the clergy of that city[1]. One accusation against him was that he had introduced methods of chanting which were unknown in the days of Gregory Thaumaturgus. The other and more serious charge concerned the ascetics who looked up to Basil as their leader. He defends them against calumnies, but admits that in comparison with the great achievements of the ascetics in Egypt, Palestine and Mesopotamia, things in Pontus are still in an undeveloped stage. His next words are significant: " If any charges of disorder are brought against the life of our women, I do not undertake to defend them." It looks as if the movement in Pontus had been accompanied by ebullitions of fanaticism which had earned the conscientious disapproval of many citizens of Neo-Caesarea. But Basil was no more responsible for the excesses of his followers than was Eustathius for most of the excesses condemned by the Council of Gangra.

The final period of Basil's career may be treated more briefly. It is full of colour and incident, but does not add much to the conclusions already reached. In 365 reports reached Caesarea that the Emperor Valens was on his way to the city, determined to wreak vengeance on its recalcitrant inhabitants. Eusebius the archbishop yielded to popular clamour and recalled Basil, the only man who seemed capable of dealing with such a crisis. With the aid of Gregory of Nazianzus a complete reconciliation was effected between the bishop and the priest. As it turned out, Valens' purpose was frustrated by the necessity of quelling the revolt of Procopius, and Basil was able to spend five years in Caesarea as Eusebius' subordinate, loyally upholding his authority and increasing the powers of the see considerably.

The outstanding event during this period was the great famine of 368, of which Basil gives an account in his homily *On the Famine and Drought*. He did all in his power both by example and precept to relieve the distress; he sold his own possessions and bought provisions with the proceeds[2],

---

[1] *Ep.* 207; cf. 210.
[2] Greg. Nyss. *In laud. Bas.*; *In Eunom.* I. 10; cf. p. 45.

and also made eloquent and successful appeals to the rich
citizens to follow his lead.

In 370 Eusebius died. Basil had been the power behind
the throne for some years, and now felt, not without justification, that the interests of the Church demanded his succession
to the vacant see. With the help of some scheming he gained
his ends, and his remarkable career as archbishop of Caesarea
began. The most famous incidents of his episcopate are the
blow which Valens struck at Caesarea in 371 by the division
of Cappadocia and creation of a new province of *Cappadocia
Secunda* with its civil and ecclesiastical centre at Tyana; the
visit of the Emperor Valens to Caesarea in 371 and 372;
Basil's quarrel with his old friend Gregory; his irreconcilable
feud with Eustathius; and his unsuccessful efforts to induce
the Western Church to interest itself in the troubles of the
East. On January 1st, 379 Basil died[1]. Though only
50 years old, he was prematurely aged by his austerities
and incessant activities, to which his physique, always frail,
was quite unequal. The funeral was an occasion for a great
display of popular affection and respect, and the honours of
sainthood were given him at once[2].

In Pontus Basil had organised a monasticism that was
already in existence. The same holds good of Cappadocia
and Caesarea. Gregory's words make it quite plain that
monasticism was well known in Nazianzus; besides the
traditional life of asceticism lived in the world, the eremitic
life was also practised. He would have adopted the solitary
life himself, had it not necessitated the giving up of sacred
study[3]. The monks of Caesarea were a powerful body in 362;
Gregory calls them "the Nazarites of our day," and says they
were enraged at the manner in which "their chief" Basil was
insulted, and would have caused a schism had not Basil retired
to Pontus[4]. Basil's letters are full of references to the monks
and ascetics of both sexes that abounded in Cappadocia and
the neighbouring provinces. These would seem to have been

---

[1] See Schäfer, *op. cit.* pp. 30, 31, for a vindication of the traditional date.
[2] Greg. Naz. *Or.* 43, 80.        [3] Greg. Naz. *Carm.* I. 65 ff., XI. 300—337.
[4] Greg. Naz. *Or.* 43, 28.

exponents of the two modes of asceticism described by Gregory, or perhaps solitaries in a modified sense, such as were called *Sarabaites* at a later period. It is possible that a form of cenobitism had already developed at Caesarea, either spontaneously, or in imitation of the institutions of Eustathius and Basil in Pontus. Basil may have taken some preliminary steps in 361 towards the foundation of his famous cenobium at Caesarea, but on the whole his personal prestige is sufficient to account for his acknowledged leadership of the Caesarean monks at this early date[1].

Sometime during the years 365—370 the foundations of the great cenobium and hospital must have been laid, because by 372 the work had attained such proportions as to alarm Elias, the governor of the province[2]. In a letter assigned to the same year the institution appears fully organised, for Basil describes one of his priests as a man of "continence and ascetic discipline...a man of poverty, with no resources in this world, so that he is not even provided with bare bread, but by the labour of his hands gets a living with the brethren who dwell with him[3]." Basil's voluminous correspondence contains many letters on the subject of the ascetic life. The impression gathered from them agrees in all essentials with the accounts given by his contemporaries, and also with the evidence of the Rules. These letters reveal a ceaseless activity in furthering the cause of monasticism and maintaining a high standard of religion among the ascetics. Where Basil cannot visit the monks in person he sends deputies[4]. Even so distant a land as Palestine is not outside his range, for in a letter to Epiphanius he mentions that he has written to the monks of the Mount of Olives[5]. He intercedes with the assessors of taxes and asks that favourable consideration may be given to the monks, from whom payment can hardly be expected[6]. In one letter he urges the

[1] Maran (*Vit. Bas.* VI. 2) says that Basil during his presbyterate sent a postulant to Pontus for instruction, which chows that he was not satisfied with the facilities for asceticism provided in Caesarea. But *Ep.* 23, from which this is deduced, says nothing about Pontus.

[2] Bas. *Ep.* 94.

[3] *Ep.* 81.     [4] *ib.* 226.     [5] *ib.* 258.     [6] *ib.* 284.

adoption of the common life, and refers to a visit he has lately paid in person in order to enforce this lesson. "Great is my desire to see you all united in one body, and to hear that you are not content to live a life without witness; but have undertaken to be both watchful of each other's diligence, and witnesses of each other's success[1]." Much interesting information is given in the "canonical" letters to Amphilochius (188, 199, 217), especially on the subject of the monastic profession. It is a debated question whether or not Basil recognised permanent *vows*, but certainly in the case of women the profession was irrevocable[2].

One of Basil's chief aims was to *organise* the monastic life. He ordains that the profession of men is not to be recognised unless they have "enrolled themselves in the order of monks," and that a careful examination must precede their profession[3]. However, from the way in which he phrases his recommendations ("I do not recognise," "I think it becoming") it may be deduced that he is speaking only for himself and that other methods existed. He evidently intended his organisation to be a step forward; stricter discipline was possible now, "since by God's grace the Church grows mightier as she advances, and the order of virgins is becoming more numerous[4]." Basil condemns private vows, such as that of abstinence from swine's flesh, as unnecessary and ridiculous[5]. The supreme importance of orthodoxy in his estimation may be seen in his decision that vows made by heretics are not binding, and may be broken without sin[6].

In conclusion, Basil's famous philanthropic institutions deserve a brief notice. Charity was far from unknown in the pagan Empire; besides the public distributions of corn to poorer citizens there were various methods of relieving distress by public and private benevolence[7]. But the Christian Church practised it with far more zeal and thoroughness, so

---

[1] *Ep.* 295; cf. *Ep.* 23.    [2] See Additional Note A.

[3] *Ep.* 199, Can. XIX.

[4] *ib.* Can. XVIII. But Cappadocia and Pontus were backward in comparison with the lands of the East. (*Ep.* 207.)

[5] *Ep.* 199, Can. XXVIII.    [6] *ib.* Can. XX.

[7] Cf. Lecky, *History of European Morals* (ed. 1911), II. 75 ff.

that Julian recognised in this one of the chief sources of its strength[1]. In the fourth century the need for charity had increased. The resources of the State were less, and the proportion of the free proletariat to the whole population was greater, now that the supply of fresh slaves had dried up and many of the existing ones had been emancipated. The Church of Alexandria had won honourable distinction for the extent of its charities, and Basil had doubtless learned much from his visit to Egypt[2]. But in this as in other respects he improved on his teachers, and his foundation at Caesarea both struck the imagination of his contemporaries and served as a model for similar institutions in other centres. Eustathius' foundation at Sebaste for strangers and invalids, presided over by Aerius, probably served to some extent as a pattern[3]. In 372 Basil wrote to the governor of the province, to whom he had been denounced, a letter on the subject[4], from which we learn that there was a magnificent church, with houses attached for the bishop and clergy. Around it was a complex of buildings for benevolent purposes, including apartments for travellers and wards for the sick. Gregory in a rhetorical description of the place states that it was outside the city and of sufficient importance to be called the New City[5]. In the collection of Basil's letters occurs one from Heraclidas to Amphilochius. Heraclidas had been in Caesarea and, not wanting to stay in the city, had gone to live in the neighbouring hospital; there he had come under the influence of Basil, who instructed him on apostolic poverty. He urges Amphilochius to join him[6]. The hospital then was a place where the ascetic life could be lived, and, though there is no definite statement to this effect, it seems clear that Basil's cenobium was also part of the same pile of buildings. This conclusion is supported by what Sozomen says of Prapidius,

---

[1] Cf. Harnack, *Expansion of Christianity*, I. 181—249.

[2] See Palladius, *Hist. Laus.* VI., for a description of the hospital at Alexandria; the men's ward was on the ground floor, the women's ward above.

[3] Cf. Epiphanius, *Haer.* 75.

[4] *Ep.* 94.

[5] Greg. Naz. *Or.* 43, 63. Queen Helena erected a Church at the Holy Sepulchre outside Jerusalem which she called New Jerusalem, Socr. *H.E.* I. 17.

[6] *Ep.* 150.

one of the most celebrated of Cappadocian monks. He " performed the episcopal functions in several villages (i.e. was a chorepiscopus). He also presided over the Basileias, the most celebrated hospice for the poor. It was established by Basil, bishop of Caesarea, from whom it received its name in the beginning, and retains it until to-day[1]." In fact one of Basil's main objects must have been to provide an outlet for the practical activities of his monks of the Common Life. It is to be noted how the tradition of Basil is continued in Prapidius, who is at once monk, bishop and philanthropist. Basil set up a working alliance between the official Church and monasticism, a fact which proved of great importance for the later history of the Eastern Church.

The example of the capital was followed throughout the province, and the chorepiscopi under Basil's direction established similar hospitals in their own districts[2]. Altogether the prestige of the Church must have been enhanced considerably by these measures. Some interesting remarks of Sir W. M. Ramsay will form a fitting conclusion to this chapter. " Such establishments constituted centres from which the irresistible influence of the Church permeated the whole district, as, centuries before, the cities founded by the Greek Kings had been centres from which the Greek influence had slowly permeated the country round[3]." And again: " such a Christian ecclesiastical establishment took the place of the ancient Anatolian *hieron* as the centre of social and municipal life. The Greek conception of a free people governing itself without priestly interference was dying out, and the Asiatic conception of a religion governing in theocratic fashion the entire life and conduct of men was reviving[4]."

---

[1] *H.E.* VI. 34.

[2] Bas. *Epp.* 142, 143.     [3] *Church in the Roman Empire* (5th ed.), p. 461.

[4] *Luke the Physician*, p. 153. Cf. *Ch. in Rom. Empire*, p. 464 n. " The ' New City ' of Basil seems to have caused the gradual concentration of the entire population of Caesarea round the ecclesiastical centre, and the abandonment of the old city. Modern Kaisari is situated between one and two miles from the site of the Graeco-Roman city." See also *Enc. Brit.* art. " Caesarea," " A portion of Basil's new city was surrounded with strong walls and turned into a fortress by Justinian; and within the walls, rebuilt in the 13th and 16th centuries, lies the greater part of Kaisarieh."

# CHAPTER V

## ST BASIL'S ASCETIC WRITINGS[1]

BASIL'S Rules are a source of considerable importance to the student of fourth century Church life, but very little use has been made of them hitherto by historians. Their fate has been unfortunate; as Holl has pointed out, the fact of their being Rules at all has given them a bad reputation, and misleading analogies, such as the history of the Franciscan Rules, have had a disturbing effect on modern criticism[2]. Even when authors have made use of them, they have generally felt it necessary to sound a note of caution in view of the probable presence of later elements. So great an authority on the history of monachism as Zöckler declares that none of the Rules in their present form go back to Basil[3]. Perhaps therefore the writer of a widely-used text-book on Church History is not to be blamed if he gives such a seriously misleading note as the following: "None of the 'Rules' ascribed to names of the fourth century (they are collected

---

[1] Garnier's discussion in the Benedictine edition is the foundation of all subsequent work. See also Ceillier, *Histoire Générale*, VI. 161—195. A brief discussion by E. F. Morison in *Ch. Quart. Rev.* Oct. 1912, repeated in his book *St Basil and his Rule* (1912), pp. 15—19, is of some importance because the writer's conclusions are based on a study of the ascetic writings from a lexical point of view, undertaken for the purpose of the forthcoming Lexicon of Patristic Greek. A book entitled *Saint Basile-le-Grand, ses œuvres oratoires et ascétiques*, by Vasson (Paris, no date), might be passed over in silence but that its title might prove attractive. It is wholly uncritical and in spite of its 752 pages contains nothing of value.

[2] Holl, *Enthusiasmus und Bussgewalt*, p. 157.

[3] *Askese und Mönchtum*, p. 286. He adds however that they are "ihrem wesentlichen Inhalte nach basilianisch." Meyer, *Die Haupturkunden für die Geschichte der Athosklöster*, p. 7, assumes amplifications by later hands in the shorter Rules. Moeller however says, "The shorter Rule may with greater confidence be regarded as his work" (*History of the Christian Church*, Eng. tr. I. 360).

by Holstenius, *Codex Regularum*) are in their original form.
They are believed to have been modified under the influence of
later experience. Two bear the name of Pachomius and two
that of Basil of Caesarea. The shorter of the latter, ὅρος κατ'
ἐπιτομήν, is regarded as nearly representing Basil's own work[1]."
But it is obviously improper to put Basil's Rules, which can
be shown to have existed in their present form within twenty
years of his death, in the same category as those of Pachomius.
We hope to be able to show, not only that they are essentially
Basilian, as indeed is generally acknowledged at the present
time, but also that any editing they may have received was
as honest a piece of workmanship as that which is carried out
in modern times by the literary executors of a dead author.

Few literary works of antiquity have better external
attestation than Basil's *Ascetica*. In *Ep.* 22 (*On the Perfection
of the Life of Solitaries*) Basil refers to a writing that he will
be able to leave behind dealing with questions raised by the
monks and based upon a study of Scripture. "I have only
deemed it necessary to speak by way of brief reminder concerning the questions which have been recently stirred among
you, so far as I have learned from the study of the inspired
Scripture itself. I shall thus leave behind me detailed evidence,
easy of apprehension, for the information of industrious
students, who in their turn will be able to inform others[2]."
The description will suit either the Morals or the Longer
Rules—the Shorter are not based on Scripture to the same
extent as the Longer. Gregory of Nazianzus recalls the
"written Rules and Canons" over which Basil and he had
collaborated[3]; he praises Basil's "legislation written and
unwritten for the monastic life[4]"; also his care for the convents,
and the "written regulations" by which he subdued every

---

[1] Rainy, *The Ancient Catholic Church*, p. 295. The two sets of Basil's Rules
are *not* in Holsten's collection, only Rufinus' conflation and condensation of them.
ὅρος is presumably a misprint for ὅροι.

[2] At an earlier period (*Ep.* 9) Basil was determined not to publish his
views.

[3] *Ep.* 6, ὅροις γραπτοῖς καὶ κανόσι.

[4] *Or.* 43, 34, νομοθεσίαι μοναστῶν ἔγγραφοί τε καὶ ἄγραφοι; cf. 43, 29,
καθιστᾷ τι μνήμης ἄξιον.

sense and regulated every member[1]. Jerome writing in 392 states that Basil composed a work "On Asceticism[2]." Rufinus, who had been Jerome's companion, returned to Italy from the East in 397 and translated "this work" (*hoc opus*) of Basil into Latin for Urseius, abbot of Pinetum. The work referred to by Rufinus, and probably by Jerome also, is the Longer and Shorter Rules of Basil, which Rufinus abbreviated and adapted so as to form one composite work[3]. A few years later we have Cassian's description of the Rules: "Basil and Jerome...the former of whom, when the brethren asked about various rules and questions, replied in language which was not only eloquent but rich in testimonies from Holy Scripture[4]." Sozomen mentions the existence of an ascetic book inscribed with Basil's name, adding indeed that some attributed it to Eustathius of Sebaste[5]. After such an amount of early testimony it seems needless to enlarge on the later allusions, or do more than mention the evidence of Justinian[6] and Benedict[7]. That of Photius is however most important and must receive some attention.

It will have been noticed that the above references attest either an undefined body of ascetic writings, or else definitely the Rules. It is clear then that the Longer and Shorter Rules are the best authenticated of the ascetic writings. A fuller discussion is necessary before the external evidence valid in their case can be transferred to other documents.

The chief witness for the textual history is Photius, patriarch of Constantinople in the latter half of the ninth century. He was quite the best-read man of his time and had an extensive acquaintance with both Christian and Pagan literature. These are his words on the subject of this chapter. "We read also *the Ascetica,* or counsels on ascetic behaviour; anyone who directs his life according to these will dwell in the heavenly kingdom." "We read the so-called *Ascetica* of

---

[1] *Or.* 43, 62, τὰ ἔγγραφα διατάγματα.
[2] Τὸ ἀσκητικόν, *De vir. illust.* 116.
[3] Rufin. *Praef.* (in Holsten, *Codex Regularum*); cf. *H.E.* II. 9, "Basilii instituta monachorum." See Appendix B.
[4] *Inst. Praef.*      [5] *H.E.* III. 14. See Appendix A.
[6] *P. G.* LXXXVI. 977.      [7] *Reg. Ben.* 73.

L. C.      5

St Basil, Bishop of Caesarea in Cappadocia, in two books....
Now his first book describes what is the cause of the great
discord and dissension in the Churches of God and in the
relations of each man with his neighbour, and with what
danger it is fraught; secondly (it shows) that transgression of
every commandment of God receives a great and terrible
punishment—with proof from the Scriptures; thirdly it
describes our pious faith, or rather our pure and sincere
confession of the Most Holy Trinity. While the second book
expresses as it were the character of a Christian in different
sections and concisely, and again by the side of this the
character of the leaders of the Word. Next it expounds
some ascetic rules, put in the form of question and answer, to
the number of 55, and again, in more concise form, other
rules, 313 in number[1]."

Basil's *Ascetica* therefore, at the time of Photius, existed
in two volumes, the first a very small one containing the two
sermons known as *De Iudicio Dei* and *De Fide*[2], and the
second a bulky volume, since it included the *Moralia* and
both Longer and Shorter Rules. Besides these we have in
our present editions the three opening writings of the *Ascetica*,
(1) *Praevia Institutio Ascetica*, (2) *Sermo Asceticus, De Renuntiatione Saeculi*, (3) *Sermo de Ascetica Disciplina*; two treatises,
both entitled *Sermo Asceticus*, which come between the Morals
and the Longer Rules; and finally the *Poenae in Monachos
Delinquentes* and the *Constitutiones Monasticae*. The absence
from Photius of this latter group of documents is, so far as it

---

[1] Photius, Cod. 144 (Migne, CIII. 422), Ἀνεγνώσθη καὶ τὰ Ἀσκητικά, ἤγουν
ἀσκητικῆς πολιτείας ὑποθῆκαι, καθ᾽ ἅς τις βιοὺς τὴν οὐράνιον οἰκήσει βασιλείαν.
Also Cod. 191 (CIII. 634), Ἀνεγνώσθη τοῦ ἐν ἁγίοις Βασιλείου, ἐπισκόπου Καισαρείας
Καππαδοκίας, τὰ λεγόμενα Ἀσκητικὰ ἐν δυσὶ λόγοις...ὁ μὲν οὖν πρῶτος αὐτῷ λόγος
διεξέρχεται τίς ἡ αἰτία καὶ ὁ κίνδυνος τῆς τοσαύτης τῶν Ἐκκλησιῶν τοῦ Θεοῦ καὶ
ἑκάστου πρὸς τὸν ἕτερον διαφωνίας τε καὶ διαστάσεως. Δεύτερον ὅτι πάσης ἐντολῆς
Θεοῦ παράβασις σφοδρῶς καὶ φοβερῶς ἐκδικεῖται. καὶ ἡ ἀπόδειξις ἐκ τῶν Γραφῶν.
Τρίτον περὶ τῆς εὐσεβοῦς πίστεως ἡμῶν, ἤτοι τῆς εἰς τὴν ὑπεραγίαν Τριάδα καθαρᾶς
ἡμῶν καὶ εἰλικρινοῦς ὁμολογίας. ὁ δὲ δεύτερος οἷον χαρακτῆρα Χριστιανοῦ κεφαλαιώδη
καὶ σύντομον παρατίθεται, καὶ χαρακτῆρα πάλιν παραπλήσιον τῶν προεστώτων τοῦ
λόγου. εἶτα οἷον ὅρους τινὰς ἀσκητικούς, ὡς ἐν ἐρωτήσει καὶ ἀποκρίσει προηγμένους,
ἐκτίθεται, τὸν ἀριθμὸν νε΄, καὶ πάλιν συντομώτερον ἑτέρους ὅρους τιγ΄.

[2] Photius' first point is found in the opening words of *De Iudicio Dei*, his
"secondly" in the main part of the same, while his "thirdly" describes *De Fide*.

goes, unfavourable to their authenticity. This concludes our survey of the external evidence; let us now proceed to the internal. It will be convenient to use the following arrangement of the writings.

A. Certainly genuine. Photius' first volume.
  (i) *De Iudicio Dei.*
  (ii) *De Fide.*

B. Certainly genuine. Photius' second volume.
  (i) *Moralia.*
  (ii) *Regulae Fusius Tractatae.*
  (iii) *Regulae Brevius Tractatae.*

C. Probably genuine, but to be used with caution.
  (i) *Praevia Institutio Ascetica.*
  (ii) *Sermo Asceticus, De Renuntiatione Saeculi.*
  (iii) *Sermo de Ascetica Disciplina.*

D. Probably spurious.
  2 *Sermones Ascetici* (placed after *Moralia*).

E. Certainly spurious.
  (i) *Poenae in Monachos Delinquentes.*
  (ii) *Constitutiones Monasticae.*

## A. (i) *De Iudicio Dei.*

This sermon or treatise "On the Judgment of God" may have been originally included in the *Ascetica* in virtue of some tradition of its having been originally addressed to monks, but more probably because, the *Moralia* having become associated with the Rules, this treatise with its companion *De Fide*, referring as they do to the *Moralia*, formed a fitting preface to the composite volume. The style is clearly that of Basil, and the biographical references at the beginning put the matter beyond doubt. The writer refers to his Christian upbringing, his travels and education, and proceeds to describe the state of the Church, which was as if "there was no king in Israel." He then reaches his main subject, the judgment of God on sin, which he works out in characteristic fashion with a wealth of Scriptural proof. His closing words are: "I have deemed it fitting and necessary first to set forth the sound

faith and pious doctrine in regard to the Father and the Son
and the Holy Spirit, and then to add the Morals[1]."

## (ii)   *De Fide.*

This is the promised doctrinal treatise; like the last, it
throws no light on the special subjects of our inquiry.  Basil's
purpose is to lay a firm doctrinal foundation before proceeding
to practical questions.  He expounds the true doctrine of the
Trinity, and then sketches the method of procedure to be
adopted in the *Moralia*.  His "brethren in Christ" have been
claiming the fulfilment of his promise to write something.  He
informs them that he has already been active in the matter,
and has written out rules of conduct, with illustrations from
the Bible; he has used the New Testament primarily, and the
Old Testament where it agrees with the New.  There is
nothing to show whether the "brethren in Christ" are monks
or Christians living in the world, or to fix the date of this
group of writings with any accuracy.  Maran gives 361 as the
date, and this is probably approximately correct, but his
arguments are not very cogent[2].

## B.   (i)   *Moralia.*

These "Morals" ($\tau\grave{\alpha}$ $\mathring{\eta}\theta\iota\kappa\acute{\alpha}$) begin at once without further
preface, showing their close organic connection with the two
preceding tracts.  They consist of 80 rules, some of which are
broken up into many different heads.  Thus Rule 70, dealing
with the duties of the clergy, has 37 sub-divisions.  The treatise
as a whole is concerned with the duties of Christians at large,
and clergy living in the world, while the "Rules" proper have
in mind the special needs of monks[3].  Basil's method is to
enunciate a proposition and then to buttress it with proof-texts

---

[1] Basil contrasts the Church distracted by its divisions with a swarm of bees he
once saw "following their own king in good order."  The idea of a bee-hive may
well have been in his mind in working out the details of his cenobia.  Cf. the
Cappadocian Elpidius who lived with the brethren "like a little king in the midst
of the bees" (*Hist. Laus.* XLVIII. 2).  See Ramsay in Hastings' *D.B.* v. 116 b for
the part played by the bee in Anatolian religion.

[2] *Vit. Bas.* VII. 3.   Ceillier, *Histoire Générale*, VI. 171.

[3] The same word ($\mathring{o}\rho o\iota$) is used for the regulations in each case.

from the Scriptures. He deals with the material in the same manner as in the "Rules," and displays a deep knowledge of both the letter and spirit of the Bible. There is little that bears on the subject of monasticism; the few passages that refer to the organised ascetic life agree closely with the evidence of Basil's other writings. Thus, money assigned to those who are consecrated to God is not to be spent on others[1]. Married people may not separate unless one has been taken in adultery, or the union has proved a hindrance to godliness[2]. There are some interesting passages on the necessity of pastoral care and visitation[3].

## (ii) *Regulae Fusius Tractatae.*

These Longer Rules (ὅροι κατὰ πλάτος) consist of 55 sections or chapters, mostly concerned with specially monastic problems. The answers are nearly always supported by proof-texts from Scripture[4]. The opening words of the preface throw light on the circumstances under which the book originated. "Since by God's grace we are assembled together in the name of our Lord Jesus Christ—we who have set before ourselves one and the same object of the life of godliness; and you are plainly eager to hear somewhat of the things pertaining to salvation, while I am bound to declare the judgments of God...and since the present time is most suitable and this place provides quiet and complete freedom from all external distractions, let us join in prayer together...." The place seems then to have been a monastery. The hearers, whose eagerness is thus described, are referred to again on several occasions in the headings to the chapters. For instance, at the head of the seventh chapter we read: "since your words have convinced us that a life in company with those who despise the commandments of the Lord is fraught with danger, we should consequently like to know whether...[5]." The heading is usually in the form of a question, direct or

---

[1] *Mor.* 31; cf. B. 187 (see p. 82).     [2] *Mor.* 73; cf. F. 12 (see p. 84).
[3] *Mor.* 70, cap. 12 and 18.
[4] The exceptions are F. 13, 26, 27, 38, 39, 49, 51, 53, 54.
[5] The heading assumes a similar personal form in F. 1, 2, 3, 24, 38, 43.

indirect, but titles such as *Concerning Slaves* (11) or *Concerning the Girdle* (23) are also found. The style is thoroughly Basilian, if not quite up to Basil's usual level of excellence[1].

We have already seen that the external attestation of both sets of Rules is very strong. A still further testimony to the originality and early date of the Longer Rules is provided by the references in the Shorter, where on three occasions Basil refuses to discuss questions because answers have been already given in the Longer Rules[2]. It may be inferred that the Longer Rules were already in circulation and accessible to Basil's hearers by this time. When we add that both style and contents are thoroughly consistent with the evidence of Basil's undisputed works, the case for the authenticity of these Longer Rules becomes overwhelming[3].

It is not difficult to fix their date within a year or two. Everything points to some monastery in Pontus as the scene of their delivery. The references in the Shorter Rules demand an interval of time between the two publications, long enough to enable the first set of Rules to be copied and circulated. It is tempting to identify the Longer Rules with the "written rules" which Gregory and Basil drew up in concert. But Gregory's sixth letter, which speaks of these, is describing his first stay in Pontus[4], and the Longer Rules can hardly be assigned to the opening months of Basil's monastic life; they presuppose a later stage of development[5]. Besides, they are not *Rules* at all, strictly speaking, but rather "conferences" or instructions on the ascetic life[6]. It is better to suppose

---

[1] For proof see Garnier, Vol. II. XI. 6. Cf. Ceillier, *Histoire Générale*, VI. 178, "Ces Règles sont écrites d'un stile un peu différent des autres ouvrages de saint Basile. Il y a moins d'élégance, moins d'élévation ; mais c'est que la simplicité convenoit à un ouvrage de ce genre."

[2] Thus B. 74 refers to F. 7, B. 103 to F. 27, B. 220 to F. 33 (cf. also B. 2 and F. 8). The answer in B. 103 is περὶ τούτων εἴρηται σαφῶς ἐν τῇ πλατυτέρᾳ ἀποκρίσει.

[3] See Chapter VI. for a description of their contents.      [4] See p. 49.

[5] E.g., in the regulation that there must not be more than one monastery in any one κώμη (F. 35). Even if, as seems almost certain, Basil organised an already existing monasticism (see p. 46), his reputation during his first retirement would not have been developed sufficiently to allow him to speak with such authority.

[6] Pargoire calls them "lectures spirituelles" or "conférences" (art. "Basile"

that Basil made a draft of Rules in 358—359 with Gregory's
help, which formed the basis of these later instructions; the
date of their delivery will then have been some time during
the years 362—365. A later date is improbable; there is
nothing to suggest that Basil was a bishop at the time, or
even that he was a priest, practically governing the Church of
Caesarea in the name of Eusebius.

If the arguments in favour of these Rules are so weighty,
how have they come to be viewed with suspicion? Possibly
owing to a wrong interpretation of the evidence of Rufinus,
who makes no use of any after the 24th. But his copy can
hardly have stopped short at this point, for up to this its
order was identical with that of our modern editions, and
various causes may be suggested to account for his neglect of
the later Rules[1]. The copy presupposed by Basil in the
Shorter Rules refers on two occasions to the part of the
Longer Rules unused by Rufinus[2].

In the time of Photius however copies existed in which
the Rules were distributed differently. In the passage quoted
above[3], the number is given as 55. But the 5 is not apparently
original and has been added in the MS by a later hand[4]. As
Tillemont says, the division of the great Rules as we have it
in our edition does not surely come from the author, but from
some unintelligent person, who out of a single one has often
made several[5]. To investigate the question thoroughly would

in *Dict. d'Archéol. chrét.*). The "conference" is a specially French institution, for
which there is no English word. Bodley, *France* (ed. 1902), p. 452, describes it as
"a lucid exposition adorned with happy illustration, and moulded in conversa-
tional form." Zöckler calls them: "Katechismen mönchischer Tugend- und
Pflichtlehre"; Morison (in *Ch. Quart. Rev.* Oct. 1912) speaking primarily of
the Shorter Rules says: "They have no more order than a series of 'Answers to
Correspondents' in a modern newspaper."

[1] See Appendix B.
[2] B. 103 refers to F. 27, B. 220 to F. 33.
[3] p. 66.          [4] See Garnier, Vol. II. XXXVI.
[5] *Mémoires*, IX. Art. XXII. Both Tillemont and Ceillier (*Histoire Générale*,
VI. 177), apparently referring to the same fact as Garnier, say that before Photius
MSS existed in which there were only 40 articles. Garnier in his *Monitum* at the
head of the *Ascetica* says: "Regulae in aliis codicibus alio ordine disponuntur.... Ad
Regulas quidem quod attinet, eas eodem ordine quo iam vulgatae sunt in editione
Parisiensi, edendas curabimus." I cannot find that he gives any further informa-
tion as to the extent of variation in the order, or whether both Longer and Shorter

require a study of the manuscript evidence that has been impossible to me ; but on a general view all that seems to be demonstrated by this is a certain amount of later editing, which indeed is probable on other grounds. The Longer Rules read like extempore discourses, and they were probably taken down in shorthand and subjected to some revision, perhaps by the author himself, perhaps by a literary executor. If the latter hypothesis is correct, the personality of such an executor is not far to seek. Gregory of Nazianzus had himself assisted in the drafting of sketch rules, he acted as Basil's literary executor in the case of the *Hexaemeron*, and, if the reports of his friend's discourses were incomplete, there were traditions of his "unwritten" regulations upon which to draw[1]. But there is no evidence to show that any elements of importance were added after Basil's death.

### (iii)  *Regulae Brevius Tractatae.*

In his preface to the Shorter Rules[2] (ὅροι κατ᾽ ἐπιτομήν) Basil refers to the circumstances of their delivery. He begins by mentioning the "gift of teaching" and "ministry of the word" with which he has been entrusted. In fulfilment of this it is his duty not only to preach publicly in Church, but also to give facilities in private, so that individuals can consult him about their difficulties. " If then," he proceeds, "God has gathered us together here, and we have complete quiet from external distractions, let us not apply ourselves to any other business, nor give our bodies up to sleep again, but let us spend the remaining part of the night in careful examination of necessary things." We gather that Basil was now bishop of Caesarea and was holding a congress of monks,

Rules are equally subject to it. F. 53 is found in B. in one codex, and is absent altogether in another, see Garnier *in loc.*

[1] Shorthand writers were widely employed in antiquity, e.g. by Origen (Eus. *H.E.* VI. 23). Eustathius of Sebaste had a number of them, whom he placed at Basil's disposal on one occasion (ταχυγράφοι, Bas. *Ep.* 223). Basil's *Hexaemeron* were apparently delivered extempore (see end of Hom. VIII) and put into shape after his death by Gregory (Socr. *H.E.* IV. 26).

[2] While the answers are much shorter than in the Longer Rules, the book itself is considerably longer, occupying nearly twice as much space in Garnier (ed. 1839); pp. 457—562 are devoted to F., 563—753 to B.

perhaps in the cenobium at Caesarea. I put forward the suggestion that this was a kind of General Chapter of the Superiors of monasteries, who were responsible not only for their own monks but also for the discipline of the attached sisterhoods. It is difficult to imagine that the abbesses were present on an equal footing with the abbots—this would have involved an amount of travelling and mixing with men such as were quite alien to the spirit of fourth century asceticism. So a question such as " If a sister will not sing psalms, ought she to be compelled to do so[1]? " must have been asked by a monk. Now Basil had already ordered that periodical meetings of Superiors should be held[2]. Was not this one of these Chapters?

What has been said above about shorthand reports applies here with equal force. Only in this case there was no editing; the notes have been transcribed and made into a book without the slightest attempt after order or arrangement. If Basil's death supervened soon afterwards, it would account for the fact that the report was not submitted to the author for revision. Zöckler characterises the present order as " almost incredible[3]." It is certainly surprising. Thus 280—282 deal respectively with the meaning of " pure in heart," the problem of a sister who will not sing, and the meaning of " We have eaten and drunk before Thee." But this very lack of order is a strong proof that we have before us a *bona fide* record of real answers to real questions. The Longer Rules are only answers to questions to a limited extent, but the practical, often trivial, nature of the questions in the Shorter Rules guarantees their originality. After Basil's death copyists would have shrunk from affixing the name of the saint to such a medley, unless in so doing they had the support of a strong tradition.

As in the case of the Longer Rules, so here the style is thoroughly Basilian, and there can be no doubt that the two are by the same author[4]. The last 27 Rules are absent in

---

[1] B. 281.  [2] F. 54; see p. 103.
[3] *Askese und Mönchtum*, p. 287.
[4] See Garnier for the linguistic proofs, Vol. II. pp. xlv—lxviii.

some MSS, but the omission is of little consequence, as the
missing portion is already represented in Rufinus[1]. A large
percentage of the questions have nothing to do with the
ascetic life, but are concerned with Scriptural difficulties, for
instance, What is Raca? (51), Who is "the meek?" (191),
What is, Charity doth not behave itself unseemly? (246). The
contents are quite as valuable for our knowledge of the life of
the monasteries as those of the Longer Rules; the next
chapter will contain an account of their evidence.

## C.

The three short tracts now to be considered do not seem
to be attested by any ancient author, nor were they in the
edition that lay before Photius. As external evidence is
wanting, we are thrown back upon the internal character of
the writings. The style, at any rate of the second and third
tracts, agrees with that of Basil's acknowledged works[2], and
the fact that they have never been attributed to any other
author is of some weight. The picture of the monastic life
given here corresponds in all essentials with the evidence of
the Rules, but adds nothing of importance to our knowledge,
so that it may be safely disregarded in summing up Basil's
conception of monasticism.

(i)  *Praevia Institutio Ascetica* (Ἀσκητικὴ Προδιατύπωσις).

This sermon, for such it is, is dominated by one thought
only, that the monk is the true soldier of Christ. The preacher
begins by describing the soldier's life of hardship, at the beck
and call of his officers, ready to march in any direction,
deprived of worldly joys and family life. The lot of the
ascetic is similar. He must shun physical marriage and be
content with spiritual marriage and the begetting of spiritual
children. For him, as for the soldier, a crown of victory is
waiting. In this army women are not rejected for their bodily

---

[1] See Appendix B.
[2] "Legi et relegi has lucubratiunculas, in quibus nihil omnino inveni, quod
indignum esset nostro Basilio." Garnier.

weakness: indeed some virgins have even surpassed men in the struggle and won greater fame. Holl is inclined to suspect this tract because it harps continually on one thought, whereas Basil's style is generally marked by a rich profusion of images[1]. But it would be unreasonable to expect a preacher to be always at his best.

### (ii) *Sermo Asceticus, De Renuntiatione Saeculi*[2].

This is a longer document, and of some importance. Its agreement with the Rules is striking and leaves little doubt that both are the work of the same author.

Basil urges his hearers to come to the cross-bearing life of the monks, divesting themselves of their riches by giving to the poor[3], and of their sins by confession[4]. But those who wish to come must first prove themselves and count the cost, lest by a subsequent apostasy they bring scandal on the Church. God has divided men into two classes, virgins and married, that those who cannot endure the struggle of virginity may live with their wives. But holiness must be practised in the married state, love of God and one's neighbour being required from all. But, he proceeds, thou who lovest the angelic life must join the monks, disregarding the protests of relations and bestowing all thy goods on the poor. This is victory in the first round. Now it is important to find a man equipped with all the necessary virtues to be thy guide in the new life; having found him, cast out all self-will and put thyself wholly in his hands. But in the second round of the contest the devil will tempt thee to leave the ascetic life and thy strict master. Resist the temptation, a lenient guide is worse than useless. Remember that by the rules of the

---

[1] *Enthusiasmus und Bussgewalt*, p. 158. Morison (*St Basil and his Rule*, p. 15), while accepting the two next writings, says this " can hardly be attributed to Basil." I see no reason why it should not be, but the data are not sufficient to warrant a definite decision.

[2] Batiffol (*La littérature grecque*, p. 256) evidently confuses this and the next discourse with the spurious ones that follow. In his list of the non-Photian works he omits the two latter and describes the two present ones wrongly as " 2 λόγοι ἀσκητικοί, l'un sur la renoncement au monde, l'autre sur la discipline ascétique, tous deux suspects, et que rien ne rattache au reste de la collection."

[3] B. 85, 92; see p. 81.   [4] F. 26; see p. 96.

contest thou wilt not be crowned unless thou hast striven
"lawfully." Therefore obey thy master; to do things apart
from him is theft and sacrilege, even if they seem to thee
good in themselves[1]. Seek no amelioration of hardship, either
in bedding or clothing or food. Be as silent as possible.
Imitate those who have made progress in virtue. Do not
judge the faults of others, but attend to thine own. Shrink
from observation. "Hast thou gone out from thy cell? Thou
hast deserted continence." But, if compelled by necessity to
go into the world, go clad with the armour of God, and return,
like the dove to the ark, the moment the business is completed[2]. If thou art young, shun the company of other young
monks whether at table or in the dormitory; even at prayers,
when a young man is opposite thee, do not look up at him[3].
Beware of gluttony[4]. Other faults are curable, but I have
never known a man cured who was gluttonous or ate in
secret. Do not sit down before an elder[5]. Reply when
spoken to, at other times be silent. Do not cross thy legs.
Eat with the right hand, and use the left only to assist the
right. Take care to sing at the divine office, and do not
depart before the end. Tame thy body and make it subser-
vient to the soul. The devil will tempt thee with bodily pain.
Do not say "Alas my head!" or "Alas my stomach!" and
use the pain to excuse absence from prayers. When it is thy
turn to serve, join words of exhortation to thy care for the
body, and treat the patient as if he were Christ[6]. Beware of
thinking that all who live in a cell will be saved. Many come
to this holy life, but few really bear its yoke. If thou hast
the rank of a cleric[7], let it not elate but rather humble thee;
and still more so if thou art raised to the priesthood. Practise
daily self-examination. Be prepared to stay in thy cell not
only for days and months but for many years.

---

[1] F. 28; B. 303; see p. 93.    [2] F. 44; B. 311; see p. 99.
[3] Cf. Zöckler, *Askese und Mönchtum*, p. 205, for similar regulations in
Pachomian monasteries.
[4] F. 18; B. 71, 131, 132, 134.    [5] F. 21.
[6] This refers to works of mercy in the adjoining hospital; cf. B. 155, 286; see
p. 100.
[7] B. 231; see p. 102.

(iii)  *Sermo de Ascetica Disciplina, Quomodo*
*Monachum Ornari Oporteat*[1].

This is a short address, recounting the notes of a monastic
life in a number of short sentences quite devoid of any
literary style. Some are epigrammatic and vigorous, such as
" to keep his eyes down and his soul up." Among the recommendations may be noted the following—to wait on invalids,
to wash the feet of the saints, to practise hospitality and
brotherly love, to read orthodox but to shun heretical books,
to avoid meeting women or using wine.

## D. 2 *Sermones Ascetici.*

The style of these is somewhat different from that of the
foregoing; in the case of technical monastic words there is a
serious divergence from the language of Basil's genuine works[2].
The precepts for the monastic life are with one or two exceptions thoroughly in agreement with the Rules, even more so
than the tracts just mentioned. The resemblance is often so
close, that one is tempted to regard these two sermons as
having been written at a later period on the basis of the Rules.
The general tendency is to give instructions on points of detail
where the Rules lay down a general principle, or else leave
the matter in the hands of the Superior. The first sermon
contains two important details : the monastery is not to have
less than ten monks, and the hours of prayer are to be seven
in number. Only six are prescribed, but the mid-day prayer
is divided into two parts with dinner in between, so that the
canonical seven hours may be attained and David's words,
" Seven times a day do I praise Thee," fulfilled. It is conceivable that Basil might have relaxed his earlier rule of eight
times of prayer[3], but in the light of differences of style it is

---

[1] The *Revue Bénédictine* (1910), p. 226 ff., contains a critical text of a Latin
version of this treatise.

[2] The gathering of the brethren is called συνοδία, συσκηνία, πλήρωμα (none of
which titles are used in Basil's genuine works); the Superior is καθηγούμενος,
προηγούμενος, προκαθηγούμενος. ἡγούμενος, the usual word for the abbot in later
times (common in the *Constitutiones Monasticae*), does not occur in the Rules.

[3] See pp. 86, 87.

preferable to suppose that these tracts were composed at a somewhat later date, perhaps in monasteries living after the Basilian model.

### E.   (i)  *Poenae in Monachos Delinquentes.*

These are plainly spurious, since they contain a number of later technical terms that are not in the genuine Basil, such as Archihebdomarius, Hesychast and others.  Besides, Basil's method in the Rules is to leave doubtful points of discipline to the discretion of the Superior, contenting himself with broad principles.  In this list of penalties each offence has its definite punishment.

### (ii)  *Constitutiones Asceticae.*

The voice of modern criticism has been uniformly unfavourable to the Constitutions.  They consist of 34 sections, some of considerable length.  They are quite unworthy of Basil in style, and are often very verbose and involved. Garnier gives a list of examples in which the language differs from that of the Rules, the different words used for the Superior being the most striking instance[1].  The tone is also different in some important particulars.  While the Rules are whole-hearted in their recommendation of a common life[2], the author of the Constitutions evidently lived at a time when the common and solitary life existed side by side, and considered them equally legitimate types of monachism.  Another mark of a later date is the relaxation of the rules about journeys[3]. The monk may now go out to visit other brethren, to do them good, or even to dissipate tedium.  The Constitutions clearly belong to a later stage of monasticism; their author must remain anonymous.

Garnier has attempted to show that they were composed by Eustathius of Sebaste[4].  His main argument is that, according to Sozomen, there was a tradition that Eustathius " was

---

[1] ὁ ἡγούμενος and compounds in Constitutions, ὁ προεστώς and ὁ πρεσβύτερος in Rules.

[2] See p. 92.                         [3] See p. 99.

[4] So Zöckler (*op. cit.* p. 287), "wahrscheinlich von Eustathius v. Sebaste."

the author of the ascetic treatises commonly attributed to Basil of Cappadocia[1]"; the Rules can be proved to be by Basil; the Constitutions are clearly not Basil's work; therefore they must be ascribed to Eustathius. But a far more natural conclusion is that Sozomen refers to the Rules, which were so widely known in the fifth and following centuries and so influential, not to the obscure Constitutions[2]. His other argument is that Sozomen's description of Eustathius' ascetic work is an accurate delineation of the Constitutions: " He became the author of a zealous discipline, both as to what meats were to be partaken of or to be avoided, what garments were to be worn and what customs and exact course of conduct were to be adopted[3]." But the description is couched in general terms, and bears no more resemblance to the Constitutions than to any other ascetic treatise.

---

[1] *H.E.* III. 14.  [2] See Appendix A for a fuller discussion.
[3] *H.E.* III. 14.

# CHAPTER VI

THE Rules as a whole, in spite of some textual difficulties and the possibility of editorial revision, may be accepted as substantially Basil's work—such was the conclusion reached in the last chapter. The present chapter will be devoted to a description of their contents, and owing to the wealth of relevant material will have to be somewhat lengthy. The data may be arranged under the following heads[1].

I. *Joining the monastery.*
  (*a*) *Withdrawal from the world.*
  (*b*) *Renunciation of possessions.*
  (*c*) *Admission to the community.*

II. *Life in the monastery.*
  (*a*) *The principle of the common life.*
  (*b*) *Prayer.*
  (*c*) *Meals.*
  (*d*) *Clothing.*
  (*e*) *Work.*

III. *Order and Discipline.*
  (*a*) *The officers.*
  (*b*) *The senior brethren.*
  (*c*) *Leaving the monastery.*
  (*d*) *Confession.*

---

[1] For practical purposes the two sets of Rules may be taken as one authority. Nothing is gained by giving them separate treatment. I have been unable to detect any substantial development in Basil's teaching in the later (shorter) Rules.

IV.　*Various other points.*

(*a*)　*Earthly relationships.*

(*b*)　*Journeys.*

(*c*)　*Charitable work.*

(*d*)　*Educational work.*

V.　*Relations with outside world.*

(*a*)　*The official Church.*

(*b*)　*Neighbouring monasteries.*

(*c*)　*Convents of women.*

VI.　*The Biblical foundation.*

I.　*Joining the monastery.*

(*a*)　*Withdrawal from the world.*

God's commandment is the one supremely important thing.
If He calls us, everything else, even love of parents, must be
renounced[1]. Spiritual retirement is essential, but this will be
found impossible apart from physical retirement, since the
sights and sounds of the world are bound to distract one from
prayer, nor can sufficient leisure be obtained for devotional
duties. Besides, contact with sinners injures the soul; their
company makes us familiar with a low standard of life and
complacent with our own moderate attainment of virtue[2].

(*b*)　*Renunciation of possessions.*

If we may judge from the attention which Basil gives to
the question of property, it would seem that many of his
disciples were men of good position, so that it was necessary
to give definite instructions as to the disposal of worldly possessions. The postulant must part with his goods on joining
the monastery, for no private property is allowed[3]. Not that
earthly things are bad in themselves—if they were, they could

[1] F. 8.

[2] F. 6. The preceding sentences are an abstract of this answer. This is the
case in the references throughout the chapter, except in the places, which should
be clear enough, where comments of the writer are inserted.

[3] B. 85.

L. C.　　　　　　　　　　　　　　　　　　6

not be God's creation—but they distract the soul from the service of God[1]. Goods must be disposed of, therefore, but with great care. They are consecrated to the Lord and must not be treated negligently. The ascetic will give them to the poor himself, if he has the requisite experience; if not, he will enlist the services of trustworthy friends[2].

Such was the ideal, but it is clear that it was interpreted in practice with great freedom, for:

(i) Basil's own renunciation was only relative. He enjoyed the income of at least part of his estate during his lifetime[3].

(ii) The possibility of property being retained is contemplated in the Rules. Relations are bidden to give the monk his income and deduct nothing, lest they incur the guilt of sacrilege. The monk is warned not to spend the money before the eyes of his brethren, for that would be invidious. But the bishop of the diocese in which the monastery lies, if he can be trusted, is to be asked to dispense the goods at his discretion[4]. It sometimes happened that a monk was able to contribute to the expenses of the brotherhood. Basil repudiates with scorn the idea that by doing so he makes himself entitled to preferential treatment[5].

(iii) In *Epistle* 284 Basil writes to the assessor of taxes, submitting to him the proposition that men who have "neither money to spend nor bodily service to render in the interests of the common weal, should be exempted from taxation. For if their lives are consistent with their profession, they possess neither money nor bodies; for the former is spent in communicating to the needy...." This shows that the absence of money was not absolute. The monks had money, but spent it on the poor; and there were cases perhaps where they did not live up to their profession of poverty[6].

The business connected with the renunciation of property sometimes produced family quarrels. It was doubtful who

---

[1] B. 92.  
[2] F. 9.  
[3] *Ep.* 37; see p. 45.  
[4] B. 187; cf. B. 94; F. 9.  
[5] B. 308 (τοῦτο ὅλον τὸ ἐρώτημα ἀνθρώπινον).  
[6] The individual monks are in Basil's mind. It would seem an anachronism to think of the taxation of a monastery as a corporate body at this early period.

was responsible for paying the taxes, and the relations were hard pressed by the Exchequer officials. Basil sanctions no evasions. Caesar must have his due. The matter should be quite simple; if the monk has retained his property, he must pay. If he has left it to his relations, clearly it is their duty[1]. If such disputes arise, the monk must not resort to secular tribunals in order to get his rights, nor on the other hand may he resist, if he is cited to appear in court[2]. It is within the province of the Superior to accept voluntary gifts from relations on behalf of individual monks, though Basil had rather he did not, for the practice is apt to cause trouble[3]. Generally speaking, Basil deprecates the reception of anyone whose attention will be occupied by the claims either of relations or the tax-gatherer; it is not safe for a man who has once entered the convent to have the care of external affairs[4]. We conclude then that where the family was favourable to the step and took responsibility for meeting the demands of the State, there was no reason why an allowance should not be made to a monk. But Basil wishes to exclude the interference of the outside world within the walls of the cloister, and forbids any enjoyment of property that infringes this principle. In this matter then he speaks with two voices. There is a great difference between this result and the position with which we started, that no private property is permissible. The divergence between the ideal and the real will be a sufficient explanation, and besides here, as elsewhere, we must remember that we are dealing with answers to particular problems, rather than Rules in the proper sense of the word[5].

### (c) *Admission to the community.*

As a general rule applicants are to be accepted, but only after a careful investigation into their character and past life. Suitable exercises of probation must be imposed, and special care exercised where the previous life has been bad, or the

---

[1] B. 94.    [2] F. 9.    [3] B. 304, 305.    [4] B. 107.

[5] In any case, it was assumed that the monk only retained his property for charitable purposes. We can imagine cases where a man enjoyed a share of the family estate which it was impossible to realise on joining a convent.

applicant of high rank[1]. The whole community is to be cog-
nisant of the admission of a new member[2]. Extra precautions
should be taken if a man applies to be admitted for a limited
period; he may be genuine, but is perhaps a spy[3]. At what
age, it is asked, may applicants be admitted? At any age, if
orphans, or if parents bring them; though in the latter case
there must be many witnesses of the transaction. But the
profession of virginity is to be delayed till years of discretion.
This will be the opportunity for sending back those who do
not care for the things of the Lord. To strengthen the resolve
of the newly enrolled, and to avoid subsequent reproaches if
they fall away, the church authorities are to be present as
witnesses when the profession is made[4]. Special regulations
are given for the cases of married people and slaves. If a
married person comes, it must be asked whether consent is
mutual. If so, the person may be received before a number
of witnesses. Even if one party dissents, the maxim "In
peace hath God called us" may perhaps justify separation[5].
Slaves who apply must be sent back to their masters, unless
indeed a wicked master has forced his servant to act contrary
to God's law, in which case we must either encourage the
slave to bear the sufferings that will be his lot for obeying

---

[1] F. 10; cf. F. 15.  No time limit is prescribed for this noviciate.

[2] B. 112.

[3] B. 97. The word used for reception ($\pi\rho\sigma\delta\acute{\epsilon}\chi\epsilon\sigma\theta\alpha\iota$) is the same as in
B. 112. In such a case the thought of permanent vows is excluded, see
Additional Note A.

[4] F. 15. In *Ep.* 199 (Can. XVIII.) 16 or 17 is given as the age of discretion.
At the Trullan Council (692) the age was reduced to 10 (Can. 40).

[5] F. 12. The ambiguity of the original (1 Cor. vii. 15) is reproduced in the
answer. The general drift is strongly in favour of the view that one party could be
received even if the other was unwilling. Basil concludes however by saying that
he has noticed many cases where the unwillingness was overcome by means
of fasting and prayer. Most writers, e.g. Garnier (*in loc.*) and Ceillier (*Histoire
Générale*, VI. 180) interpret this to mean that the reception was only provisional
and was annulled if the prayer was unavailing. Such an interpretation is unlikely
for (*a*) the answer in itself reads differently; (*b*) the decrees of Gangra, directed
against Eustathius, show that such cases of separation existed and caused great
scandal (Basil owed much of his ascetic teaching to Eustathius); (*c*) in *Mor.* 73
Basil says married people are not to separate unless one is taken in adultery,
*or hindered in godliness*; (*d*) F. 11 allows the reception of slaves in a similar
case.

God rather than man, or else receive him and endure the troubles entailed by such a course[1].

Very little is said about the discipline to which novices were subjected. Silence is mentioned as especially suitable for them, in order that they may, by uttering nothing except in the Church services, learn the manner of speech proper to the religious life and forget old bad habits[2]. They are to make a point of learning passages of Scripture by heart[3].

## II. *Life in the monastery.*

### (a) *The principle of the common life.*

The cenobitic form of monasticism was deliberately adopted by Basil in preference to the eremitic or quasi-eremitic. He justifies his choice in language which deserves high praise for its eloquence and clear insight into the spirit of Scripture. Man is a social animal, he declares, and we are all dependent one upon another. Love of our neighbour is implanted naturally in our hearts. Christ teaches us the identity of our neighbour with Himself, and the love of Christ and of our neighbour pass and re-pass into one another[4]. The cenobite is better than the anchorite for the following reasons.

(i) We are none of us self-sufficient in the matter of providing for our bodily needs.

(ii) Solitude is antagonistic to the law of love, since the solitary is bound to serve his own interests.

(iii) It is harmful to the soul, when we have no one to rebuke us for our faults.

---

[1] F. 11. It is generally said (e.g. by Nissen, *Die Regelung des Klosterwesens*, p. 18) that Basil ordered slaves to be sent back to their masters. But though Basil quotes the case of Onesimus, his main point lies in the concluding sentence. If his advice was followed it must have caused great friction. The question was dealt with at Gangra (Can. 3), and the Council of Chalcedon forbade the reception of a slave into a monastery without the master's leave (Can. 4). Cf. Greg. Naz. *Ep.* 79 ; Jer. *Ep.* 82, 6.

[2] F. 13.                       [3] B. 95.

[4] F. 3. τίς οὖν οὐκ οἶδεν, ὅτι ἥμερον καὶ κοινωνικὸν ζῷον ὁ ἄνθρωπος, καὶ οὐχὶ μοναστικὸν, οὐδὲ ἄγριον; Cf. Epict. *Diss.* II. 10, who speaks of man as ζῷον ἥμερον καὶ κοινωνικόν. Basil introduces the phrase as a well-known saying. Note his significant description of man as "*not a monastic* animal."

(iv)  Certain specific Christian duties, such as feeding the hungry and clothing the naked, are impossible for the true solitary.

(v)  We are all members one of another and Christ is our Head.  If we separate from our brethren, how can we keep our relation to Christ intact?

(vi)  We have different spiritual gifts.  The solitary buries his one gift, but in a cenobium each shares in the gifts of the brethren[1].

(vii)  Most important of all, the solitary is in danger of self-pleasing, and thinking he has already attained perfection. In the nature of things he cannot practise humility, pity or long-suffering[2].

The cenobitic being the perfect form, it is also the final form.  There is no place for any return to the eremitic life. If a man wishes to secede from the community and lead a solitary, or even a quasi-solitary, life with a few others, Scripture justifies the brethren in excluding him from their number. Every such act of self-pleasing is alien to the true spirit of piety[3].

## (b)  Prayer[4].

In the religious life there is a time for work and also for prayer.  It is true every time is suitable for prayer, yet a man must not be allowed to shirk labour under the pretext of devotion[5].  The morning, on waking from sleep[6], is to be the first hour of prayer, in order that the first movements of the soul may be consecrated to God.  At the third hour the brethren, who will have dispersed to their various tasks, are summoned together; they recall the gift of the Holy Spirit at this hour and pray for His help.  If any are too far away to

---

[1] It is important to notice Basil's conception of his monasteries as possessing charismatic gifts.

[2] F. 7.  Basil does not see that his arguments prove too much, and can applied equally well to a Christian life in the world.

[3] B. 74.  There is another possible interpretation, see Additional Note B.

[4] See Morison, *St Basil and his Rule*, pp. 58—71.

F. 37.

One monk was set apart for the task of waking the others, see B. 43, 44.

come, they must say their offices wherever they find themselves. Mid-day is the next time according to the tradition of the saints[1]. Psalm xc. (xci.) will be recited, as a protection against the special temptations of the noonday. Next comes the ninth hour, the apostles' time of prayer[2]. At the close of day we thank God for the blessings of the day and seek pardon for sins committed. As night comes on we ask God for a rest "without offence and free from phantasies," and repeat Psalm xc. (xci.) once more[3]. The example of Paul and Silas and the words of the Psalm[4] teach us that midnight is a necessary time of prayer. Again, in accordance with the same psalm[5], we rise before dawn to pray. None of these times may be neglected; the ever-varying course of psalmody and prayer helps to destroy evil desires and keep the attention alert[6].

Such is the daily scheme of prayer. The interesting feature in it is the presence of two night offices, midnight and early morning. The latter is clearly not to be identified with the first of the series, for one comes before, the other after the final sleep. Basil then prescribes eight canonical hours. This conclusion is borne out by what we read elsewhere of his broken sleep[7], and also by the way in which he avoids quoting the obvious verse "Seven times a day do I praise Thee[8]." In keeping with this spirit of prayer the utmost gravity of demeanour must be preserved. Quiet smiles are permitted, but no laughter, for Christ is never recorded as having laughed[9].

Frequent communion was no doubt the rule. Basil's own practice was four times a week, and oftener if a saint's day

---

[1] Ps. liv. (lv.) 17.          [2] Acts iii. 1.

[3] In the Compline of the Western Church the same psalm is used. Cf. the thought of the office hymn, *Procul recedant somnia et noctium phantasmata, hostemque nostrum comprime, ne polluantur corpora.*

[4] cxviii. (cxix.) 62.          [5] cxviii. (cxix.) 148.

[6] F. 37.

[7] *Epp.* 2, 207; Greg. Naz. *Or.* 43, 61; Greg. Nyss. *In laud. Bas.*

[8] It is actually quoted in *Serm. Asc.* 322 A, where however only six offices are given. In order to make up the requisite number of seven, Sext is divided into two halves, before and after the mid-day meal. The authenticity of this tract is doubtful, see p. 77.

[9] F. 17; B. 31.

occurred[1]; while the usual Egyptian custom was to partake
on Saturday and Sunday. Besides the references to priests in
the monastery[2], which presuppose the exercise of priestly
functions, there are a few passages which show that regular
communion was the practice. Instructions are given how to
prepare the soul for reception[3]. The Lord's supper is not to
be celebrated except in a church, unless under very exceptional circumstances[4]. As a general rule therefore each
monastery had its own church[5].

### (c) Meals.

Basil's aim was to avoid any extremes of asceticism. On
his first retirement to Pontus he had practised great austerities,
and the Rules show a distinct reaction from his original
standpoint. In the same way did Benedict, after spending
three years as a young man in the severest self-mortification,
prescribe for his followers a studiously moderate rule of life.
One passage would lead us to suppose that the mid-day meal
(τὸ ἄριστον) was the only one during the day, since the penalty
for being late without good cause is to go hungry till next
day[6]. But elsewhere supper (τὸ δεῖπνον) is mentioned by the
side of the other meal[7]. Probably, as in the Benedictine Rule[8],
the evening meal was of such modest dimensions that it in no
way made up for the loss of the mid-day meal. There is to
be a fixed order at meal times and one is to be responsible for
the seating[9]. A book is to be read, and the brethren are to
think more of what they hear than of what they eat[10]. Food

---

[1] See *Ep.* 93, where he approves of daily communion. The custom of the
solitaries, he says, was to take the sacrament into the desert with them and partake
of it when they so desired.

[2] B. 64, 231, 265.　　　　　[3] B. 172.

[4] B. 310; cf. B. 309, and perhaps B. 122, where however "the blessing" of
which the monk is deprived for a penance is probably not the Eucharist. See
Lucot's note on *Hist. Laus.* xxv. 3, "benedictionem, liberalité, aumône ; *Onom.*
p. 443, *eulogia*: cibaria benedictionis gratia transmissa, signum communionis et
charitatis."

[5] This applies also to the convents of women; certainly Macrina's convent had
a church, see p. 50.

[6] B. 136. In *Serm. Asc.* (322 A) the meal is fixed definitely at the sixth hour.

[7] F. 21.　　　　[8] C. 39.　　　　[9] F. 21.　　　　[10] B. 180.

must be simple, cheap and easily prepared, such as is in common use in the district. Thus bread and fish are appropriate, since with these our Lord fed the multitude. Nothing beyond water is to be drunk, unless it be a little wine for health's sake[1]. The monks must not be dainty or greedy, but must eat what is set before them[2]. If a monk wants more food, or food of better quality, owing to hard work, a journey or sickness, the authorities at their discretion may give it him[3]; he must not ask for it himself on the ground of fatigue[4].

We find here a general standard of moderate asceticism prescribed for all the monks. Basil sets his face against individual austerities and condemns anything that makes a monk unable to eat the ordinary food[5]. Self-imposed fasts are forbidden. To fast or watch more than the rest is self-will and vain-glory. No extra austerities may be attempted unless good reasons for doing so have been given to the authorities and their sanction obtained[6].

### (d)  Clothing.

As soldiers and senators wear a uniform, so it is fitting that monks should dress alike. Useful garments are to be worn that will serve for night as well as day. A separate night garment is not as a rule allowed, though hair-cloth may be worn for purposes of mortification[7]. Biblical examples point to the necessity of a girdle[8]. Shoes are to be chosen for their plainness, cheapness and serviceableness[9]. It is sinful to treat either clothes or shoes in such a way that they wear out prematurely[10]. All articles of apparel are obtained from the authorities of the monastery and must be accepted with humility. If they are too coarse or too old, the monk will reflect that they are more than he deserves. But if they do not fit, he may modestly point out the defect[11].

[1] F. 19.         [2] F. 18; B. 71, 131—134.
[3] F. 19.         [4] B. 135.        [5] B. 129.        [6] B. 137, 138.
[7] F. 22; B. 90.  [8] F. 23.         [9] F. 22.         [10] B. 70.
[11] B. 168.

### (e)   Work.

Basil's regulations on this subject are characteristic and interesting. Work, he says, is ordered by Scripture. It keeps the body under control and provides necessaries for the weaker brethren. The life of the monastery is to be regarded as one continual round of work, not only with the hands, but also with the heart and tongue in the daily offices[1]. The spirit in which work is performed is most important. The monk must bear in mind that he is working to satisfy, not his own needs, but those of others[2]. Thus, in advocating the claims of work, Basil is careful not to weaken the true ascetic spirit. For himself the monk has no anxiety as to food or clothing, but trusts in God. So necessary is a right intention that the products of a man's labour are to be rejected, if his work is done in a rebellious or murmuring spirit[3]. When a novice joins the community, the Superior is to decide his work and what trade, if any, he is to learn[4]. A monk cannot decide such matters for himself, but falls in with whatever the authorities judge best for him[5]. He is to do just what he is told and not shirk heavy tasks[6]. Nor may he do more of his proper work than is commanded; this is self-will, and the man may be punished by having his work taken from him[7]. Tools must be kept carefully and regarded as dedicated to God[8]. The work is done for the most part in workshops under the direction of a foreman; strangers are rigidly excluded, and even members of the community whose work lies elsewhere[9].

Basil is asked to define the trades that are fitting for a convent. He declares that the answer will depend to a large extent on local circumstances, but as a general rule the trades should be such as suit a quiet life, have a ready market for their wares, do not require meetings of men and women, and minister to necessity rather than luxury or vice. Weaving, shoemaking, building, carpentering and metal-working satisfy

---

[1] F. 37.            [2] F. 42.                  [3] F. 29.
[4] B. 105.          [5] F. 41; B. 117, 119.       [6] B. 121.
[7] B. 125.          [8] F. 41; B. 143, 144.       [9] B. 141.

these requirements, but the best of all is agriculture, since it ties down the labourers to one place[1]. In the case of agriculture it was no doubt easy to dispose of the produce in supplying the needs of the community or in gifts to the poor[2]. But in the case of the workshop it was often necessary to seek a market for the wares. Basil directs that goods are to be sold near at hand, whenever possible, even though this entails accepting a low price[3]. For journeys are contrary to the spirit of monastic life and ought to be avoided. If however a journey becomes inevitable, carefully chosen men are to be sent, who will keep one another up to the mark and observe the hours of prayer on their travels[4]. But in choosing markets care must be taken to avoid the fairs which take place at "synods." Such meetings ought to be for prayer and praise only. The cleansing of the temple by our Lord teaches the wrongfulness of the commercial element on such occasions[5].

The more educated among the monks may be set apart for intellectual work, especially the study of the Scriptures. They form a privileged class among the brethren, and it is their duty to know as much as possible. The Superior decides who is to take up this line of work[6].

---

[1] F. 38.    [2] Or in supplying the neighbouring convent of women, see p. 105.

[3] F. 39. Cf. *Reg. Ben.* c. 57, which orders that goods are to be sold at a lower price than that demanded by secular workmen—a well-meant principle which has led to much trade jealousy in later times.

[4] F. 39.

[5] F. 40. Cf. *Epp.* 169—171, which describe the conduct of Glycerius the deacon (and monk), who led a band of young women in procession to the feast at Venasa. Ramsay, *Church in Roman Empire* (5th ed.), pp. 443 ff., has a most interesting chapter on this episode. He shows that in pagan times there was a great *synodos* of Zeus at Venasa, the priest of which shrine was second in importance in all Cappadocia only to the priest of Komana. He does not mention the description of the *synodos* in F. 40, where Basil tells us that it was a religious meeting at a Martyr's shrine, to which a commercial element was attached, a feature to which he objected strongly. This tells in favour of Ramsay's position. The *synodos* then was an old pagan festival to which a fair was attached. When the country became Christian, the Catholic custom of celebrations at martyrs' tombs was grafted on to the old observance. The commercial element persisted; Basil tried to break it down, but vested interests were too strong for him. Venasa is still a great sanctuary, where the Moslems venerate the founder of the Dervish order (*Enc. Brit.* art. "Cappadocia").

[6] B. 96, 105, 235, 236. Basil and Gregory compiled the *Philocalia* in their Pontic retreat, see p. 55.

### III.   *Order and Discipline.*

### (a)   *The officers.*

Basil applies the illustration of the body to his communities. Each member has his place, and it causes trouble and confusion if any one neglects his own work or usurps the function of another[1]. A number of officers are needed for the government of the monastery.

### (i)   *The Superior*[2].

As in all religious communities the Superior's position is one of great importance. There are checks on his power, as we shall presently see, but on the whole it is greater than at a subsequent period. For in later times the Rule itself becomes supreme ; it represents the voice of the founder or reorganiser and the Superior is as much bound by it as the humblest of the brethren. But before the Rule is fixed, much must be left to the discretion of the Superior. So here we find that Basil frequently lays down general principles rather than exact rules, and in several instances leaves the question open for the Superior to decide in accordance with local needs[3].

A new Superior is to be elected to his office by the heads of the neighbouring monasteries[4], and after a time of probation accepted by the brethren[5]. He ought to rule by example rather than word, to be merciful, and to lead men on to imitate

---

[1] F. 24.

[2] The Superior is designated in several different ways. I have counted the following occurrences of the various titles. In F. ὁ προεστώς 30 times, and ὁ ἐφεστώς, ὁ προκαθεστώς, ὁ προέχων, ὁ προϊστάμενος occasionally. Phrases such as ὁ ἐπιτεταγμένος (τῇ ἀδελφότητι) and ὁ τὴν κοινὴν φροντίδα πεπιστευμένος also occur. In F. 43 the office is called ἡ προστασία. In B. ὁ προεστώς occurs 17 times, ὁ πρεσβύτερος 5 times (with the corresponding titles for the head of a sisterhood ἡ προεστῶσα 2, ἡ πρεσβυτέρα 4 times), while various periphrases are also used. ὁ ἡγούμενος, the usual word in later Greek monasticism, does not occur. It is frequent in *Const. Mon.* See Besse, *Les Moines d'Orient*, pp. 167, 168, for other titles.

[3] E.g. F. 32 ; B. 105, 106.

[4] F. 43, ἐγκριθέντα τῶν ἐν ταῖς ἄλλαις ἀδελφότησι προεχόντων.

[5] F. 43, οὗτοι...δοκιμαζέσθωσαν πρῶτον, εἶτα διακονείτωσαν ἀνέγκλητοι ὄντες. Cf. B. 303, μετὰ πολλῆς δοκιμασίας.

Christ[1]. He must watch for the souls of his brethren, remembering that he will be called to account for any negligence[2]. Special watchfulness is needed when he suspects a brother of sin[3]. It is his place to define the punishments to be laid on erring monks[4], and to assign work to the brethren, setting some to manual labour, others to literary tasks[5]. The monk has made a solemn promise to obey the Superior, and he ought to interpret it literally, even though obedience should entail death[6]. It is obvious that such powers might lead to grave abuses in the hands of an unscrupulous or wrong-headed Superior. Provision is therefore made for certain checks on his power. The senior brethren, those who are first in age and understanding, are to admonish him if he goes astray[7]. Not only so, but even the rank and file of the monks must not obey him if his orders are contrary to God's commandments; they must "prove all things[8]." This is a remarkable instance of individualism in the Rules and a clear proof of their early date. No provision is made for the dead-lock that would occur if the Superior refused to accept the admonition of the elder brethren, or for a state of affairs in which the monks were disobeying their Superior's commands. In practice such problems would hardly have arisen in Basil's life-time, for, at any rate during his episcopate, he would soon have settled with an unsatisfactory abbot.

## (ii) *The second in command.*

Next to the Superior comes an officer who holds the second place. His task is to take charge during the absence of the Superior, lest "a democratic state of things" should arise, and, in particular, to represent him whenever necessary in the reception of guests[9].

---

[1] F. 43.      [2] F. 25.      [3] B. 19.
[4] B. 106.      [5] B. 96, 105.      [6] F. 28; B. 303.
[7] F. 27, τοῖς προέχουσι τήν τε ἡλικίαν καὶ τὴν σύνεσιν.
[8] B. 114, 303.
[9] F. 45; cf. *Hist. Laus.* XXXII. 8 for the "second in command" at Tabennisi.

### (iii)  *Other officials.*

The steward has charge of the commissariat, and must take special care to treat all alike and have no favourites[1]. Similarly the cellarer must divide to each according to his need[2]. If a man discharges his duty well in any office, he is not to be superseded, but he must always have someone in training to carry on his work if he is suddenly removed[3]. Reference is also made to the overseer of the workrooms[4].

The whole community takes part on occasion in the work of government; thus the whole body of the brethren has a right to be consulted about the reception or expulsion of a member and in certain matters of dispute[5]. But even where the brotherhood as a whole is mentioned as the final authority, it is suggested as an alternative that the matter should be left in the hands of the Superior[6].

### (b)  *The senior brethren.*

More important and interesting than this assembly of the whole community is a council of senior brethren. The rank and file of the brethren are told to attend to their work and not scrutinise the behaviour of the Superior. But this does not apply to the seniors, with whom the Superior is to take counsel[7]. They form a kind of governing body, charged with specific duties, for it is their place, being "first among the brethren in age and intelligence," to admonish the Superior if he does wrong[8]. Again, if a monk has a genuine grievance in connection with his tasks, he is encouraged to appeal to the seniors (τοῖς προεστῶσι). The usual meaning of the word is the head of the monastery, but as in this case the appellant monk is in the singular and those to whom he appeals in the plural, it is natural to conclude that a class of seniors or

---

[1] F. 34 ; B. 149, 150.     [2] B. 148.     [3] B. 156.
[4] B. 141, 142.     [5] F. 14, 49; B. 112; cf. 104.
[6] F. 49. The difference between the two methods seems great, and shows how far removed this is from a set of formal Rules.
[7] F. 48, ἐκτὸς τῶν ἐγγυτέρων τοῦ προεστῶτος, καὶ βαθμῷ καὶ συνέσει. Cf. B. 104—the Superior must do everything μετὰ βουλῆς.
[8] F. 27.

superiors within the monastery is in view[1]. The inferiors are
bidden to confess their sins either to the Superior, or else to
those who are charged with the pastoral care of weak souls[2].
The monks in question are not necessarily priests, but the
possessors of the requisite charismatic gifts[3]. It is tempting
to identify them with the "seniors," for these, though generally
the oldest, were not universally so[4]. There is further evidence
of the existence of a higher and lower grade within the
monastic life. The question is raised whether it is expedient
to learn much Scripture by heart. Basil replies that there are
two classes (τάγματα) in the monastery—teachers and taught.
The first, who have supremacy (προστασία[5]) over their brethren and the care of their souls, should know as much as
possible ; the others, who possess different gifts, must learn
to obey and do their own duty, faithful performance of
which will fit them for a call to higher work[6]. It is quite
clear that this refers to two grades among the monks, not to
a distinction between novices and monks. Had social distinctions anything to do with this difference of grades in
Basil's monasteries ? Men of education and good family, such
as Basil, would find in the study of Scripture and other books[7]
a work suited to their capacities. But the monastery might
contain all sorts, even slaves[8]. A slave woman could even
accompany her mistress to the ascetic life and continue her
service[9]. The manual labour would naturally fall to the lot
of such recruits It was possible to rise from one grade to the
other[10], but the higher grade may well have consisted in
practice mainly of the upper class[11].

---

[1] B. 119, εἰ δέ τινα λόγον ἔχειν νομίζει τῆς παραιτήσεως τοῦ ἔργου, φανερούτω
τοῦτον τοῖς προεστῶσι, καὶ καταλιμπανέτω τῇ ἐκείνων δοκιμασίᾳ. Another interpretation, of an appeal to a council of abbots of different monasteries, is improbable.

[2] F. 26, τοῖς πεπιστευμένοις...εὐσπλάγχνως καὶ συμπαθῶς ἐπιμελεῖσθαι τῶν
ἀσθενούντων.

[3] See p. 97.                [4] F. 27; B. 169.

[5] The same word is used in F. 43 of the position of the Superior.

[6] B. 235.        [7] B. 96, 235.        [8] F. 11.

[9] Greg. Nyss. *Vit. Macr.* (*P.G.* XLVI. 968). Cf. the relations of Naucratius
and Chrysapius (see p. 22).

[10] B. 235.

[11] I am aware that the above account raises more difficulties than it solves.
The distinction between elders and juniors in a monastery was general and natural

### (c) Leaving the monastery.

The monk has promised to obey, and his obedience must be absolute. If he persists in disobedience, in the last resort he must be expelled, the whole community sharing the responsibility of this[1]. The profession is permanent, having been made with all solemnity before God. To break it is to sin against God and commit sacrilege. To such a renegade the doors are not to be opened, not even if he is passing that way and begs shelter[2]. There are circumstances however under which a monk may leave the community without apostasy. If he has genuine grievances for which he cannot get redress, then he may leave the brotherhood, for they are no longer brothers, but strangers, whom he is leaving[3].

### (d) Confession.

For maintaining the discipline of the community Basil relies chiefly on the practice of frequent confession. The Rules are preoccupied with problems of sin and penitence to an extent quite unusual in Eastern Christendom; here as in some other respects Basil's ideas are rather such as are generally associated with the West. All sins, so he declares, must be disclosed to the Superior or senior brethren[4]. Mention

---

(see Cass. *Coll.* XVIII. 3). But this seems to go far beyond the ordinary practice. The difficulty is that, after giving such great authority to the Superior, Basil proceeds to coördinate the powers of the senior brethren with his. The Superior and seniors are designated by the same titles, as is also their office (ὁ προεστώς, ὁ πρεσβύτερος, ἡ προστασία). And yet Basil is afraid of any "democratic" developments (p. 93). The clue probably lies in conditions surrounding the early Cappadocian monastic movement of which we are ignorant (p. 46). The resemblance to the later distinction between the Great and Little Habit is only superficial. (See p. 135 for proof; the abbot belonged to the Little Habit.) A truer analogy may be found in the college of elders that made its appearance in the fourteenth century in the idiorrhythmic monasteries of Mount Athos (see Meyer, *Die Haupturkunden*, p. 2).

[1] F. 28.      [2] F. 14.      [3] F. 36; cf. B. 102.

[4] F. 26, 46. In 26 the heading has τῷ προεστῶτι, but the answer speaks of each of the subordinate monks (ἕκαστον τῶν ὑποτεταγμένων—note the singular) making confession to a class of brethren charged with this duty (τοῖς πεπιστευμένοις κ.τ.λ.).

is made of the confession of children[1], and also on the part of those who have returned to the convent after a journey[2].

To whom are sins to be confessed? There were priests in the monastery, who celebrated the Eucharist, but a careful reading of the Rules and a glance at the later history of Greek monachism lead us to the conclusion that the duty of hearing confessions was not assigned to the monk-priests as such. Basil says that, just as confession was made to John the Baptist and to the apostles, so now we confess to those "who are entrusted with the stewardship of God's mysteries[3]." The mention of the "mysteries[4]" might seem to point to the priesthood, but the form of the question ("Ought one to make confession to any and everyone, or to whom[5]?") implies that no such restriction was in common use, while the reference to John the Baptist, the typical ascetic, implies that the thought here, as in other answers, is of spiritual fitness rather than official rank. So Basil orders confession to be made to those who have the care of weak souls[6], that is, probably, the senior brethren or at least some of them. The nuns have to confess to the Superior (or senior brother) but the Mother-Superior (or senior sister) must be present[7]. Basil insists on the analogy of the physician. We do not reveal diseases to anyone, but only to those who are skilled in healing disease. Similarly we confess our sins to those who know how to heal, the strong who can bear the infirmities of the weak[8], that is, to the members of that charismatic ministry which was so striking a feature of Greek monasticism[9].

---

[1] F. 15.

[2] F. 44; cf. *Serm. Asc.* 323 C, D, where confession is ordered to be made every night if necessary.

[3] B. 288; cf. 229.

[4] "Stewardship of the mysteries" is a natural quotation from 1 Cor. iv. 1, and need not be pressed.

[5] εἰ πᾶσιν ἐξομολογεῖσθαι ὀφείλει καὶ τοῖς τυχοῦσιν ἢ τίσιν;

[6] F. 26; see p. 95.

[7] B. 110. (As ὁ πρεσβύτερος, ἡ πρεσβυτέρα are the words used, the translation "priest" for πρεσβύτερος seems to be excluded.)

[8] B. 229.

[9] On the whole subject see Holl, *Enthusiasmus und Bussgewalt beim griechischen Mönchtum.* On p. 262 he points to a passage in the *Life of Pachomius* about confession of sin, but shows that there was no formal rule on the subject. The

## IV. *Various other points.*

There are a number of points which do not come under any of the heads treated so far and may be introduced at this place.

### (*a*)　*Earthly relationships.*

The Superior must not as a rule allow the monks to visit their relations, for such visits are fraught with danger to the soul. Sometimes a monk's desire to visit his kinsfolk is prompted by anxiety to help them in their affairs, but he must not be allowed to implicate himself in worldly business. Whether a monk may see his relations when they visit the convent depends on circumstances. If they are engaged in profane life they have nothing in common with us; but if pious, they should be considered kinsmen of the whole

introduction of the duty of confession by Basil was a change of epoch-making importance, and was prompted by the same motives that led him to put the cenobitic life in the place of the eremitic. See also pp. 267, 268; confession is based on the conviction that man (1) sins constantly, at least in thought; (2) needs the help of others. The ideas are radically different from those of the official Church, and go back to Origen. He concludes that here at least the feeling is to be found that official acts are not enough to quiet the conscience, and that personal authority is needed, really to get into touch with the needs of another. The whole of Holl's fine book should be read by those who are interested. He traces the history down to Simeon the New Theologian in the eleventh century, who composed a treatise on the lawfulness of confession to non-ordained monks. The monks as "friends of God" were regarded as the successors of the prophets and martyrs. Of course not all the monks were resorted to by the Christian public for this purpose, but only such as showed by their lives that they possessed the requisite power. Simeon's opponents would have said that the power rested with the *monastic priesthood.*

Roman Catholic scholars have been puzzled by this phenomenon. Some have denied its existence. Marin however acknowledges it in a somewhat misleading way. " Parfois, il est vrai, il arriva que les abbés non revêtus du sacerdoce confessèrent leurs religieux; des abbesses même usurpèrent ce pouvoir; mais leur conduite fut souvent blâmée par les conciles" (*Les Moines de Constantinople,* p. 96).

Morison (*op. cit.* pp. 74—76) opposes Holl's view. He acknowledges the existence of confession to laymen in Clement of Alexandria and in later Greek monasticism, but denies it in Basil; "the monks would be most unwilling to incur a reputation for irregularity in their administration of the sacrament of penance."

For confession in primitive Anatolian religion see Ramsay, Hastings' *D.B.* v. 127 *b.*

community and received, if they come for spiritual edification, brethren with the gift of utterance being deputed to interview them[1]. Sometimes visitors will invite us to return home with them; if this is likely to result in the building up of their faith, it may perhaps be allowed[2]. To receive the visitors, who need not necessarily be kinsfolk, one of the brethren is set apart as guest-master. If another monk is addressed, he will remain silent and point to the guest-master. It is no more fitting for anyone to apply the healing words than for anyone to be a doctor[3]. The presence of guests is not to cause any interruption of the common routine[4], nor is any special food to be provided on such occasions[5]. It seems clear that the monasteries were generally recognised as homes of devotion in which spiritual gifts abounded; the visitors came primarily for spiritual edification[6].

### (*b*) *Journeys.*

As we have just seen, journeys are considered contrary to the spirit of monastic life. Special leave from the Superior is necessary before undertaking them, and they are not to be permitted merely for friendship's sake[7]. But sometimes a journey becomes unavoidable, in order to supply the necessities of the convent or to sell the products of the workshop. It is most important to find monks who can travel without peril to their souls—better starvation than that. If no suitable men can be found in the monastery, perhaps some brethren from a neighbouring convent may be deputed. On their return the monks must give an account of what they have done, and the Superior award praise or blame. To be obliged thus to describe all that occurs on the journey will prove a safeguard to the travellers[8].

### (*c*) *Charitable work.*

We have already seen that almsgiving is expected both at the outset of the monastic life, and, in some cases, afterwards[9].

---

[1] F. 32; cf. B. 188.     [2] B. 189.
[3] F. 45.          [4] B. 189.          [5] F. 45.
[6] Cf. *Mor.* 38, *Hex.* VIII. 5 for Basil's insistence on hospitality.
[7] F. 44; B. 189, 311.     [8] F. 44; cf. 39, 40.     [9] See pp. 81—83.

But the duty belongs to the whole brotherhood, not to the individual monk, who may not even give away his old clothes or shoes. It is not his duty to give at all, a special officer is appointed for the task[1]. This officer is described in general terms[2], but in one place he is apparently identified with the steward and bidden to take counsel with the seniors who come next to him in rank[3]. The almoner is to decide who are to be the recipients of the bounty of the community, but Basil lays down the guiding principle that what is destined for one set of recipients must not be diverted to another. The charity of the monastery is intended for those who are dedicated to God, but still, just as dogs eat of the crumbs that fall from the table, so there may be something left over for casual beggars[4].

There are surprisingly few allusions to the charitable institutions which, so we learn from other sources[5], were connected with Basil's monasteries. What is to be done, ask Basil's interlocutors, if a brother falls ill? Is he to be taken to the hospital (ξενοδοχεῖον), or, the alternative presumably is, nursed in the convent? The reply is that it must depend on local circumstances[6]. An interesting side-light is thrown on the working of these institutions by another question. When we wait upon the sick in the hospital, we are commanded to treat them as if they were the Lord's brethren. But, if their moral character makes the designation plainly inappropriate, what sentiments should we cherish towards them? Basil answers that the Superior must exhort and admonish the sinner, but, if his efforts are fruitless, in the last resort the man must be expelled[7]. So the hospital was not like a modern philanthropic institution, but was intended primarily to strengthen the influence and power of the Church, and therefore spiritual discipline had at all costs to be preserved.

---

[1] B. 87, 91.                    [2] B. 87, 91, 100, 101.

[3] B. 302, ἐν τῇ τοῦ οἰκονόμου ἀνακείσθω δοκιμασίᾳ μετὰ κοινῆς τῶν μετ' αὐτὸν προεχόντων γνώμης.

[4] B. 101, 302. The reference seems to be to a class of pious poor who expected the charitable ministrations of the convent.

[5] See pp. 60—62.            [6] B. 286.            [7] B. 155.

### (d) Educational work.

Boys (and girls[1]) are received into the monastery to be brought up in a godly manner. If orphans, they are to be regarded as the children of the whole community; if brought by parents, they may be accepted, but great care must be exercised. (In the case of girls especially there was a tendency on the part of parents or guardians to bring them in order to get them off their hands[2].) The education is to be different from that received in secular schools. A merely secular school is neither pleasing to God nor consonant with our profession[3]. The school is to be separate from the monk's apartments for the sake of both parties. The boys will not respect their elders if they see too much of them, and especially if they see them undergoing punishment. Also it is better for the monks, lest they should be troubled by hearing the sound of the boys' education. The boys are to have separate treatment in the matter of sleep and meals, but may join in the common prayers. Their master is to be a man of some age with a reputation for leniency. Punishments must be carefully chosen to fit the crime. The Scriptures are to be the main subject of instruction, so that they may learn about noble deeds rather than myths. Rewards are to be given to encourage the children. They are to be frequently questioned as to their thoughts; their simple minds will tell the truth, and they will avoid thinking of foolish things, lest they be

---

[1] The same directions apply, *mutatis mutandis*, to girls. In F. 15 we read that the apartments of the boys and girls are to be separate from those of the monks and, presumably, from one another (ἀφωρίσθαι δὲ καὶ οἴκους καὶ δίαιταν τοῖς τε ἄρσεσι τῶν παίδων, καὶ ταῖς θηλείαις, κ.τ.λ.). Butler, *Camb. Med. Hist.* I. 528, says: "orphanages were established, separate from the monasteries but close at hand and under the care of the monks, in which apparently children of both sexes were received." Nissen, *Die Regelung des Klosterwesens*, p. 16, writes, "Hier werden mehrere Gebäude vorausgesetzt, da die ins Kloster aufgenommenen Kinder, nach den Geschlechtern geschieden, von denen der Ältesten getrennte Häuser bewohnen sollen." Cf. Miss Bateson, *Transactions of the Royal Hist. Soc.*, Vol. III. (1899). None of these writers mention the nuns in this connexion. It is surely inconceivable that men looked after girls. The girls must have been attached to the female side of the double monastery.

[2] *Ep.* 199, Can. XVIII.

[3] B. 292, διδασκαλεῖον (*v.l.* διδάσκαλον) παιδίων βιωτικῶν (cf. 1 Cor. vi. 4).

detected in their folly[1]. Cases of discipline that the master cannot deal with himself must be referred to the Superior[2]. While the boys thus share in much of the convent life, they are not to make a profession until they reach the age of discretion. This will be an opportunity to send back those who do not care for the things of the Lord[3].

## V. *Relations with outside world.*

Our survey of the internal arrangements of the monastery as revealed in the Rules is now complete. It only remains to see how the individual monasteries were related to (*a*) the official Church, (*b*) neighbouring monasteries, (*c*) convents of women.

### (*a*) *The official Church.*

There is very scanty evidence on this point. The references to Communion imply the presence of priests in the monastery[4]. In one place it is asked what must be done "if a brother, or even sometimes a priest, behaves badly towards me and shows himself hostile[5]," from which it may be gathered that the monks were usually laymen. The authority of the bishop is recognised when Basil ordains that the profession is to be made in the presence of the Church authorities[6], and advises putting the disposal of the monk's property in the hands of the bishop, if he is a fit person[7].

---

[1] F. 15.      [2] τὸν ἔφορον τῆς κοινῆς εὐταξίας, F. 53.

[3] F. 15. Were these schools meant to give a general education or to train boys as embryo monks? The latter must have been the chief aim, if we may judge from Basil's answer. Where he deals with general education, as in the famous *Hom.* 22 (On the study of pagan literature, cf. also *Hom.* 12), he gives very different advice. But many must have returned to the world after their training was finished, and so indirectly the monasteries furthered the general cause of education.

[4] See p. 88.

[5] B. 231. Cf. *De Ren. Saec.* 10 (211 B); and *Ep.* 188, Can. x., which shows the aversion to ordination in certain circles.

[6] F. 15, τοὺς προεστῶτας τῶν ἐκκλησιῶν.

[7] B. 187, ὁ τὴν φροντίδα τῶν κατὰ τόπον ἐκκλησιῶν πεπιστευμένος. The word "bishop" is avoided; perhaps the uncertainty of Church affairs made Basil chary of using it.

## (b) *Neighbouring monasteries.*

The different communities form a kind of loose federation. There is no question of an "order" in the later sense, but the requirements that the Superiors should hold conferences with fixed times and places of meeting[1], and that a new Superior should be nominated by the heads of "the other brother-hoods[2]," show that the monastery was not quite an independent unit. Basil deprecates the continued existence of small communities[3], and will not allow more than one in a single parish (κώμη). Special qualities are needed in a Superior, and there are not likely to be two or three men with the requisite gifts in one and the same place. Besides, there is the danger of rivalry between the neighbours. If then there are monasteries side by side, let them be amalgamated. It will prove cheaper, for one lamp and one fire will suffice. With larger numbers the monastery becomes self-contained and there is less going out. It is a splendid opportunity for the Superiors of the suppressed convents to set an example of humility. Not only in one place, but even in larger areas, Basil would like to see the monasteries thus amalgamated[4]. The relations of the communities were not apparently all that could be desired. Basil declares it to be an intolerable state of things when one convent is poor and its prosperous neighbour does not come to its help; if one community is in distress, it should have no hesitation in applying to the others[5]. It is very doubtful whether buying or selling among brethren ought to be allowed, but, if it is done, generous terms must be given, and the buyer should be even more careful than the seller that the price is not too low[6].

---

[1] F. 54.  [2] F. 43.
[3] It is sometimes said that Basil instituted a system of small monasteries. This is only true if his cenobia are compared with some of the great Egyptian monasteries.
[4] F. 35. The *quondam* Superiors hold a place of some authority by the side of the Superior of the one monastery. Does not this help to explain the unique position of the senior brethren? See pp. 94, 95.
[5] B. 284.  [6] B. 285.

### (c) Convents of women.

It is natural to trace the system of double monasteries found in the Rules to the special circumstances of Basil's early ascetic life, and to suppose that the arrangement by which Basil and Macrina directed men and women ascetics on opposite banks of the Iris formed a pattern for later developments. But the system may have arisen quite independently; it suited the needs of married people who renounced the world together, and provided protection for the women in a rough age.

In any case we have here a regular system of double monasteries, linked by economic as well as spiritual ties. Some of the rules deal with points of discipline arising in the sisterhoods[1], and elsewhere Basil shows that he has the needs of the women in mind[2]. He is apparently addressing an audience that consists of Superiors, and perhaps senior brethren, but not of inferior brethren, who had no part in the government of the monasteries[3]. Occasionally an awkward problem arises with reference to sisters, from which we gather that the Superiors were to some extent responsible for their discipline and government. The answers make this certain. The Superior must not speak to a sister unless the Mother-Superior is present[4], and even to her he speaks as little as possible[5]. Nor may a sister confess to a Superior (or senior brother) unless the Mother-Superior (or senior sister) is present. Penances must not be imposed without her knowledge[6]. They must be varied according to the age of the offender, for young women and old have different temptations[7]. Specific problems are raised with reference to the sister who refuses to sing[8], and the stewardess who has charge of the wool[9]. The necessary conversations between the two

---

[1] E.g., B. 82, 111, 153, 281.    [2] B. 104, and the reference to girls in F. 15.

[3] See pp. 72, 73, for the circumstances under which the Shorter Rules were delivered.

[4] B. 108.                         [5] B. 109.

[6] B. 110, 111. In 108, 109 the words ὁ προεστώς, ἡ προεστῶσα are used. In 110, 111 they change to ὁ πρεσβύτερος, ἡ πρεσβυτέρα. The general supervision of the sisterhood rests with the Superior, but the power of hearing confessions with any of the senior brethren. I think however that ἡ πρεσβυτέρα means the Mother-Superior, but is altered to correspond with ὁ πρεσβύτερος.

[7] B. 82.          [8] B. 281.          [9] B. 153.

sides of the monastery will be conducted by representative senior members. Solitary interviews are forbidden, and not less than two or more than three are to be present on either side. But if others want to send or receive messages, let them do it through the agency of these senior brothers or sisters[1].

The visits of priests to the sisterhood were of course necessary for the purpose of celebrating the Eucharist; but a Rule which has been taken to refer to this is of doubtful meaning, and may be better interpreted of economic interdependence. In question 154 of the Shorter Rules it is asked, If in a double monastery the sisters are more numerous than the brothers, and the brothers have to separate for the purposes of work, is the situation free from danger[2]? The answer is, If they are unanimous in heart, they may be present spiritually, though not in body. Question and answer are alike obscure, but seem to refer to a division of labour. The men would do field work and provide food for the women, while the latter would make the men's clothes[3]. If the number of monks fell short of the normal, in order to provide for the needs of the sisterhood, they would have to be scattered at a distance from one another as they worked and the hours of prayer could not be observed properly. This is opposed to the ideals of the common life; it need not however, says Basil, break the monks' spiritual unity[4].

Double monasteries were suppressed by Justinian, and the prohibition needed to be repeated by later legislators. They were a special feature of Irish monachism, and were brought to England by the Celtic missionaries. They seem possible

---

[1] F. 33; cf. B. 220.

[2] A free paraphrase. The Greek is ἐὰν συμβῇ ὀλίγους ὄντας ἀδελφοὺς, καὶ πλείοσιν ἀδελφαῖς ἐξυπηρετουμένους, εἰς ἀνάγκην ἐμπίπτειν τοῦ διίστασθαι ἀπ' ἀλλήλων, διαμεριζομένους πρὸς τὰ ἔργα, εἰ ἀκίνδυνον τὸ τοιοῦτον.

[3] Cf. B. 112 where wool is mentioned.

[4] This seems to be Nissen's view. See *Die Regelung des Klosterwesens*, p. 10, where he speaks of a common "wirtschaftliche Grundlage." I interpret B. 154 in the light of F. 33, which speaks of conferences between the two sides over the needs of the body. But the passage is difficult and Miss Bateson's explanation may be right (*Transactions of the Royal Hist. Soc.* (Vol. III.) 1899). "The contingency is contemplated in which the number of brethren may be so small that they must serve the nuns singly" (i.e. when they visit them to conduct services). But can διαμεριζομένους πρὸς τὰ ἔργα mean this?

only at times of pure and fervent enthusiasm, and tend to be superseded by lower but more practicable ideals.

## VI.   *The Biblical foundation.*

The Rules as a whole are steeped in Scripture and most of the details of the ascetic life are regulated by Biblical texts. In nearly all the Longer Rules Basil appeals to proof texts to support his teaching, and the same is true of many of the Shorter[1]. In some places his interpretation is slavishly literal, as when he allows the brother who waits upon others to raise his voice, because "Jesus cried[2]." Monks, he says, on their return from a journey must give an account of all that they have done, for so did the saints in the Acts[3]. They have promised to obey the Superior, and must do so even unto death, for Christ was "obedient unto death[4]." The cenobium is definitely modelled on the pattern of the earliest Christian community, which had all things in common[5].

But more frequently the answer is faithful to the spirit as well as the letter of Scripture. A good example is seen in the arguments for the superiority of the common life. How is it possible to gird oneself, and wash the feet of the saints, in solitude? As we have diverse spiritual gifts, we shall be spiritually destitute ourselves unless we share in the gifts of others. How can we properly sustain our relation to Christ the Head, unless we are in union with our brethren, all living as members one of another[6]?

An even better example is found in Basil's teaching with reference to the reception of recruits to the monastic life. They are to be bidden to renounce all, as did St James, St John and St Matthew. It is perilous to reject any applicants, for Christ bade all to come. But as He tested the young man, so we must not accept anyone without probation[7]. These are but a few instances ; many more might be found. The Rules as a whole are worthy of the great Bible student who composed them.

[1] Cf. B. 1, where Basil discusses the authority of Scripture.
[2] B. 151; Jn xii. 43.
[3] F. 44.        [4] F. 28.        [5] B. 85.        [6] F. 7.        [7] F. 8, 10.

# ADDITIONAL NOTE A

## PERMANENT VOWS

The question has often been discussed whether Basil insisted on permanent and irrevocable vows in the modern sense of the term, or whether he regarded the monastic profession only as a very solemn and binding obligation laid on the individual by public opinion and his own conscience. Jackson in his translation of Basil (*Nicene and post-Nicene Fathers*, p. lii) has a learned note on the subject, and quotes de Broglie, Bulteau and Montalembert in favour of the first view; he himself questions "whether St Basil's Rule included formal vows of perpetual obligation in the more modern sense." E. F. Morison (*Ch. Quart. Rev.* Oct. 1912), considers "there would always be a difficulty in making such vows legally binding, but so far as the monastery was concerned they were to be considered irrevocable." One of the greatest living authorities on monasticism, Dom E. C. Butler, states that "a profession of virginity was made, but no monastic vows were taken....But though there were no vows, St Basil's monks were considered to be under a strict obligation of persevering in the monastic life" (*Camb. Med. Hist.* I. 528). He cites Palladius as his authority for this statement. Let us now consider the evidence, beginning with Palladius.

(1) Palladius, writing in 420, praises Lausus for his good sense in not having bound himself by a vow or oath, and thus exposed himself to the danger of perjury. (μήτε ὁρμῇ τινι καὶ προλήψει ἀλόγῳ ἀνθρωπαρέσκως ὅρκῳ πεδήσας τὴν προαίρεσιν, καθὼς πεπόνθασίν τινες φιλονείκως φιλοδοξίᾳ τοῦ μὴ φαγεῖν ἢ πιεῖν δουλώσαντες τὸ αὐτεξούσιον τῇ ἀνάγκῃ τοῦ ὅρκου, καὶ τούτῳ πάλιν ὑποπεσόντες οἰκτρῶς φιλοζωΐᾳ καὶ ἀκηδίᾳ καὶ ἡδονῇ τὴν ἐπιορκίαν ὠδίναντες. *Hist. Laus.* prol. 9, ed. Lucot.) The primary reference is to rash vows of abstinence from food and drink, such as Basil condemns in unsparing terms (Ἐκεῖνό γε μὴν γελοῖόν μοι κατεφάνη, τὸ εὔξασθαί τινα ὑείων ἀπέχεσθαι κρεῶν. ὥστε καταξίωσον διδάσκειν αὐτούς, τῶν ἀπαιδεύτων προσευχῶν καὶ ἐπαγγελιῶν ἀπέχεσθαι. *Ep.* 199, Can. XXVIII.). But while vows of virginity do not seem to be in Palladius' mind at this point, it may be gathered from the general tenor of the passage that he disapproves of them. Now the *Lausiac History* aims at giving a faithful picture of contemporary monachism; the author's verdict here must reflect a point of view that was generally prevalent.

(2) Basil's Rules. In F. 14 one who has been received into the brotherhood and then breaks his profession (τὴν ὁμολογίαν ἀθετήσαντα) is to be treated as a sinner against God; he is guilty of sacrilege, having stolen what belongs to God (ὁ γὰρ ἀναθεὶς ἑαυτὸν τῷ Θεῷ, εἶτα πρὸς ἄλλον βίον

ἀποπηδήσας, ἱερόσυλος γέγονεν, αὐτὸς ἑαυτὸν διακλέψας, καὶ ἀφελόμενος τοῦ Θεοῦ τὸ ἀνάθημα). The monastery doors are to be closed to such a one and not even opened when he begs for shelter. F. 15 treats of the profession of virginity, which is not to be exacted from children, but must be deferred till years of discretion (τότε καὶ τὴν ὁμολογίαν τῆς παρθενίας προσίεσθαι δεῖ, ὡς ἤδη βεβαίαν, καὶ ἀπὸ γνώμης οἰκείας καὶ κρίσεως γινομένην). The Church authorities are to be present as witnesses (Μάρτυρας δὲ τῆς γνώμης τοὺς προεστῶτας τῶν ἐκκλησιῶν παραλαμβάνειν, ὥστε δι' αὐτῶν καὶ τὸν ἁγιασμὸν τοῦ σώματος ὥσπερ τι ἀνάθημα τῷ Θεῷ καθιεροῦσθαι, καὶ βεβαίωσιν εἶναι τοῦ γινομένου διὰ τῆς μαρτυρίας). Cf. B. 2. Short-term vows were however allowed under exceptional circumstances (p. 84).

(3) The "canonical" letters to Amphilochius. Basil, *Ep.* 199, Can. XVIII., says that the old rule was that virgins who fell after professing virginity and thereby annulled their agreements (ἀθετουσῶν τὰς ἑαυτῶν συνθήκας) should be excommunicated for a year. But as the Church advances it is possible to make stricter rules. "It is my judgment (ἐμοὶ δὲ δοκεῖ) that careful consideration should be given to the act as it appears upon consideration, and to the mind of Scripture." The virgin is the bride of Christ, and so for her to break her profession is to be guilty of *adultery*. Professions may be made at full age, that is, 16 or 17. The girl may then be ranked among the virgins, her profession ratified and its violation sternly punished (τότε ἐγκαταλέγεσθαι χρὴ ταῖς παρθένοις, καὶ τὴν ὁμολογίαν τῆς τοιαύτης κυροῦν, καὶ τὴν ἀθέτησιν αὐτῆς ἀπαραιτήτως κολάζειν). The next Canon (XIX.) goes on to discuss the case of men. "We do not recognise (οὐκ ἔγνωμεν) the professions of men, except in the case of those who have enrolled themselves in the order of monks (τῷ τάγματι τῶν μοναζόντων) and seem to have secretly adopted the celibate life. Yet in their case I think it becoming (ἡγοῦμαι...προσήκειν) that there should be a previous examination, and that a distinct profession should be received from them, so that whenever they may revert to the life of the pleasures of the flesh, they may be subjected to the punishment of fornicators." *Ep.* 217, Can. LX., reads thus: "The woman who has professed virginity and broken her promise (τῆς ἐπαγγελίας) will complete the time appointed in the case of adultery in her continence. The same rule will be observed in the case of men who have professed a solitary life and who lapse."

(4) Basil, *Epp.* 44, 45. These are of doubtful authenticity. *Ep.* 42, to Chilo, is attributed to Nilus, see Garnier *in loc.* (In Codice Regio 2895 haec leguntur : τινὲς τὸν λόγον τοῦτον τοῦ ἁγίου Νείλου εἶναι λέγουσιν). *Epp.* 42—46 form a unity, and stand or fall together. In *Ep.* 44, to a lapsed monk, the writer speaks of agreements with God (συνθήκας) made before many witnesses. In *Ep.* 45 a lapsed monk is condemned for adultery, which need not mean more than marriage. The sinner has incurred the guilt of perjury, having inculcated vows, whereas to say more than Yea or Nay is attributed to the evil one (τὰς τῷ Θεῷ προσφυγούσας ψυχὰς φρικτοῖς ὅρκοις κατέκλεισας, ὁπότε παρατετηρημένως τοῦ ναὶ

καὶ τοῦ οὗ τὸ περιττὸν τῷ διαβόλῳ προσνενέμηται). The point of view agrees with that of Palladius rather than with Basil's opinions as found in his undisputed writings.

The most important points of the evidence have now been given; other regulations concerning admission to the Basilian community may be found on pp. 83—85. The testimony of *Epp.* 44, 45 can be ruled out; from what remains the following conclusions may be drawn.

(*a*) The profession was an exceedingly solemn occasion, led up to by careful preparation; it took place in the presence of witnesses and, if possible, before the bishop of the diocese. The professed monk was bound by Church law, public opinion and his own conscience. He incurred the guilt of sacrilege if he went back on his promise.

(*b*) In Basil's estimation the monk and nun were on a somewhat different footing. The virgin was reckoned as the bride of Christ in a sense that was inapplicable to the male ascetic. Her guilt was accordingly greater if she went back to the world. For her to marry was equivalent to adultery (cf. Nissen, *Die Regelung des Klosterwesens*, pp. 26, 27; see also Reitzenstein, *Die hellenistischen Mysterienreligionen*, pp. 21—23, for heathen parallels to this idea).

(*c*) Basil is conscious of being an innovator. He is introducing a new discipline which is only possible because of the development of ascetic principles. His mode of expression betrays the fact that his views were not generally accepted ("it is my judgment," "we do not recognise," "I think it becoming").

I infer therefore that the new principle introduced by Basil was the irrevocable nature of the profession, at least in the case of virgins. Whether or not the vow was of such a character that to violate it incurred the guilt of *perjury* is a minor question; it contained all the essentials of the vow as understood in later times. The practice of permanent vows may therefore be traced back to Basil; it had not however won general acceptance at the time Palladius wrote his *History*.

## ADDITIONAL NOTE B

### ST BASIL AND THE SOLITARY LIFE

The problem to be discussed is this; Basil put forward the claims of cenobitism in vigorous and uncompromising fashion (see pp. 85, 86), but was he consistent in his teaching and practice? In Chapter VIII. it will be shown that the Eastern Church in the following centuries valued cenobitism mainly as a preparatory stage, a kind of school in which the aspirant might learn the ascetic life, in order to practise it as a solitary as soon as he was able to stand alone. Was this position a contradiction of Basil's ideal, or merely a development of certain elements that were present, if not conspicuous, in his teaching? The relevant passages are as follows:

(1) Basil, F. 7. Dealing with the comparative merits of the solitary and common life, Basil decides in favour of the latter on every count. (See pp. 85, 86 for an exposition of his teaching.) One of his points is that a solitary has no one to correct him for his faults. "(Such a spiritual guide) it is very difficult to find in solitude, if not previously united in the life; and so in his case the saying of Scripture comes true, Woe to the solitary man, because if he fall, there is none to raise him up." (῝Ον ἐπὶ τῆς μονώσεως εὑρεῖν ἄπορον, μὴ προενωθέντα κατὰ τὸν βίον· ὥστε συμβαίνειν αὐτῷ τὸ εἰρημένον ἐκεῖνο. Οὐαὶ τῷ ἑνί, ὅτι ἐὰν πέσῃ, οὐκ ἔστιν ὁ ἐγείρων αὐτόν). Garnier's rendering of the difficult words μὴ προενωθέντα κατὰ τὸν βίον is an interpretation rather than a translation—*Si prius in vitae societatem adiunctus non fuerit*. If this rendering holds good, Basil is pointing out the difficulties which beset a solitary life, but allows that, where the solitary has previously belonged to a cenobium, this particular difficulty is obviated; the spiritual relations begun in the cenobium may be continued in solitude. Such an interpretation is flatly opposed to the rest of this answer, but it is hard to suggest a better rendering. It must be acknowledged that the vigour and passion of Basil's language go to show that his teaching on this point did not meet with general acceptance; it is possible that in practice he found himself compelled to make concessions.

(2) F. 36 treats of those who leave the brotherhood. If a monk is suffering spiritual harm and cannot get redress, then he is justified in departing. But if he leaves the convent (τῆς συναφείας τῶν ἀδελφῶν) in a spirit of levity, he is not to be received by the other brotherhoods (ἀπρόσδεκτος ἔστω ταῖς ἀδελφότησιν). No other causes of separation are to be recognised. Nothing is said about leaving the cenobium in order to seek a solitary's cell, but Basil's language seems to exclude such a course.

(3) B. 74. So far the evidence has been indirect; here the question is definitely raised whether it is permissible to pass from the common to the solitary or quasi-solitary life. "We ask to be taught from Scripture whether one ought to cut off those who go out from the brotherhood, and wish to live a solitary life, or else to pursue the same end of piety in company with a few others." (Τοὺς ἐξερχομένους ἐκ τῆς ἀδελφότητος, καὶ βουλομένους μονήρη βίον ζῆν, ἢ μετὰ ὀλίγων τῷ αὐτῷ ἕπεσθαι σκοπῷ τῆς εὐσεβείας, εἰ χρὴ ἀφορίζειν, διδαχθῆναι ἀπὸ τῆς Γραφῆς δεόμεθα). Basil in reply stigmatises all self-will as impious, and refers to his fuller treatment of the subject in the Longer Rules. The reference must be to F. 7, which is one long panegyric of the common life. Zöckler, *Askese und Mönchtum*, p. 288, paraphrases B. 74 thus: "Will ein Bruder gern zum einsiedlerischen Leben übergehen, so darf er dies nicht eigenmächtig, sondern nur mit Genehmigung des Vorgesetzten thun." There is no

mention of the Superior, though Basil's interrogators are probably
Superiors (p. 73). Nor is there any hint that consent might be given;
ἀφορίζειν implies an unfriendly act, and Basil's answer, though ambiguous,
does not remove the impression left by this word.

(4) *Ep.* 42. This is a letter to Chilo, a solitary, living perhaps in
Palestine. The writer bids Chilo persevere in his mode of life, and resist
as a temptation of the devil the thoughts of the world that allure him
back. "You" says the Evil One "are sitting here in a wild state like the
beasts. You see round you a wide desert with scarcely a fellow-creature
in it, lack of all instruction, estrangement from your brothers, and your
spirit inactive in carrying out the commandments of God." It seems
psychologically impossible that this letter could have come from the man
who composed F. 7, and it is probably a letter of Nilus incorporated by
accident into the collection of Basil's Letters[1].

It is only necessary for our purpose to consider the passages where
there is a contrast, implied or expressed, between the two modes of the
ascetic life. Basil mentions the solitaries or monks in a number of
places in his epistles, without however betraying whether he is using the
terms in a general or special sense. The evidence so far is inconclusive,
but on the whole the impression left by the answer of F. 7 (apart from
the words discussed above) is not seriously weakened.

We turn now to Gregory of Nazianzus, the companion of Basil in the
Pontic monastery and his collaborator in devising Rules for its government. Unfortunately, his testimony is given in so rhetorical a form that
its meaning is far from clear.

(5) The chief passage is *Or.* 43, 62. Τοῦ τοίνυν ἐρημικοῦ βίου καὶ τοῦ
μιγάδος μαχομένων πρὸς ἀλλήλους ὡς τὰ πολλὰ καὶ διϊσταμένων, καὶ οὐδετέρου
πάντως ἢ τὸ καλὸν ἢ τὸ φαῦλον ἀνεπίμικτον ἔχοντος· ἀλλὰ τοῦ μὲν ἡσυχίου
μὲν ὄντος μᾶλλον καὶ καθεστηκότος καὶ Θεῷ συνάγοντος, οὐκ ἀτύφου δὲ διὰ
τὸ τῆς ἀρετῆς ἀβασάνιστον καὶ ἀσύγκριτον· τοῦ δὲ πρακτικωτέρου μὲν μᾶλλον
καὶ χρησιμωτέρου, τὸ δὲ θορυβῶδες οὐ φεύγοντος, καὶ τούτους ἄριστα κατήλ-
λαξεν ἀλλήλοις καὶ συνεκέρασεν· ἀσκητήρια καὶ μοναστήρια δειμάμενος μέν,
οὐ πόρρω δὲ τῶν κοινωνικῶν καὶ μιγάδων, οὐδὲ ὥσπερ τειχίῳ τινὶ μέσῳ ταῦτα
διαλαβὼν καὶ ἀπ' ἀλλήλων χωρίσας, ἀλλὰ πλησίον συνάψας καὶ διαζεύξας·
ἵνα μήτε τὸ φιλόσοφον ἀκοινώνητον ᾖ μήτε τὸ πρακτικὸν ἀφιλόσοφον (ed.
Boulenger). Browne and Swallow (*Nicene and Post-Nicene Fathers*
series) translate thus: "Moreover he reconciled most excellently and
united the solitary and the community life. These had been in many
respects at variance and dissension, while neither of them was in absolute
and unalloyed possession of good or evil: the one being more calm and
settled, tending to union with God, yet not free from pride, inasmuch as
its virtue lies beyond the means of testing or comparison; the other,
which is of more practical service, being not free from the tendency to

[1] See p. 108. Nilus was a Palestinian ascetic who died in 430; for his works
see Bardenhewer, *Patrologie* (1910), p. 317.

turbulence. He founded cells for ascetics and hermits, but at no great distance from his cenobitic communities, and, instead of distinguishing and separating the one from the other, as if by some intervening wall, he brought them together and united them, in order that the contemplative spirit might not be cut off from society, nor the active life be uninfluenced by the contemplative." This version is open to grave objection. To begin with, it is most improbable that Gregory spoke in this manner of Basil's achievement. Basil's great contribution to monasticism was the establishment of community life. Could his bosom friend, in an oration almost fulsome in praise, have dismissed one of the great works of his life with a few depreciatory remarks, and then gone on to find his true significance in the fact that he instituted some hermits' cells in the vicinity of his cenobia? The antecedent improbability of this interpretation is supported by the absence of any corroboration in Basil's ascetic writings.

The key to the understanding of the passage lies in the recognition of the fact that Basil is represented as instituting a *tertium quid* by the side of two existing forms of asceticism. The first is clearly the solitary life; what is the second? Leclercq (*Dict. d'Archéol. chrét.* art. "Cénobitisme," col. 3149), supposes that Basil made a middle form between the anchorite life and that of the great Egyptian monasteries. But, so far from doing this, he developed to the full the tendency to a common life already present in Egypt. It is true μιγάς has been given the meaning "cenobite" by many good scholars (e.g. Ducange, *s.v.*, and Clémencet) but the rendering cannot be upheld. It must refer to the ascetic life lived in the world (see pp. 12, 46: cf. Boulenger, *Grégoire de Nazianze, Discours funèbres*, pp. cv, cvi). We now get an admirable sense for χρησιμώτερον and θορυβῶδες, the latter of which would be a most curious description of Basil's cenobia. The third thing that Basil made was of course the monastery of the common life; with this interpretation the passage yields admirable sense. I offer the following paraphrase of the concluding words. He founded monasteries (ἀσκητήρια and μοναστήρια are two names for the same thing—ἀσκητήριον is used in *Hist. Laus.* XVIII. 12 of Tabennisi), not far removed in spirit[1] from those who were living the "community" life (i.e., as previously understood—κοινωνικῶν and μιγάδων are two names again for the same thing, natural in a funeral oration). Nor did he separate the two modes of life as if by a wall, but combined in his own institutions the advantages of both[2].

It remains now to see whether Gregory's use of μιγάς elsewhere supports this explanation[3].

---

[1] I take πόρρω metaphorically, since τειχίῳ and πλήσιον are also figurative; but it may be literal, and mean "not far away—like the hermits' cells."

[2] Boulenger by taking κοινωνικῶν = cenobites seems to me to destroy the sense of the passage.

[3] μιγάς is used of pell-mell confusion in the classical period, and, at least in one passage, of the mixing of two opposites. See Eur. *Bacch.* 17—19, 'Ασίαν τε πᾶσαν, ἣ παρ' ἀλμυρὰν ἅλα κεῖται, μιγάσιν Ἕλλησι βαρβάροις θ' ὁμοῦ πλήρεις

(*a*) *Or.* 43, 66. Gregory asks what pleasure is left after Basil's death for the monks (μοναστῶν ἢ μιγάδων). Two classes are referred to. μοναστῶν is a general word, and is used of the cenobites in Pontus (νομοθεσίαι μοναστῶν, ἔγγραφοί τε καὶ ἄγραφοι 43, 34). The other class must therefore be the unorganised ascetics living in the world.

(*b*) *Carm.* XI. 310. Gregory describes his own choice of the ascetic life as a middle way between two extremes. (μέσην τιν᾽ ἦλθον ἀζύγων καὶ μιγάδων, τῶν μὲν τὸ συννοῦν, τῶν δὲ τὸ χρηστὸν φέρων.) He gives the sons of Jonadab and John the Baptist as examples of ἄζυγοι, and describes the μιγάδες as πρακτικοί. The parallel to *Or.* 43, 62 is very close[1].

(*c*) *Or.* 2, 29. Among the unmarried there is a great difference between the solitaries and the μιγάδες. (κἂν ἔτι ἀκριβῶς ἐξετάσῃς, ὅσον τὸ μέσον τῶν ἐν συζυγίαις πρὸς τοὺς ἀγάμους, κἂν τούτοις πάλιν, τῶν τῆς ἐρημίας πρὸς τοὺς κοινωνικοὺς καὶ μιγάδας.) Here again κοινωνικοί and μιγάδες have the same meaning. Gregory speaks of the two extreme types, not of cenobitism, which is considered a *via media*.

(*d*) *Or.* 21, 19. Athanasius, like Basil, reconciled the two modes of life. There were solitaries in Egypt, also monks who "cherished the law of love in community life, being at once solitaries and μιγάδες." (οἱ μὲν τὸν πάντῃ μοναδικόν τε καὶ ἄμικτον διαθλοῦντες βίον, ἑαυτοῖς μόνοις προσλαλοῦντες καὶ τῷ Θεῷ, καὶ τοῦτο μόνον κόσμον εἰδότες, ὅσον ἐν τῇ ἐρημίᾳ γνωρίζουσιν· οἱ δὲ νόμον ἀγάπης τῇ κοινωνίᾳ στέργοντες, ἐρημικοί τε ὁμοῦ καὶ μιγάδες). This passage is of special importance, as throwing light on the similar passage in *Or.* 43, 62. I imagine that the reference is to the visit of Athanasius to Tabennisi in 330. Relations between the two branches of monachism had been strained, but Athanasius now set the seal of official approval on Pachomius' work (see p. 39).

This note has run to considerable length, but it seemed desirable to discuss the question fully. We have found nothing in Gregory's words to upset the conclusions arrived at from a study of Basil. It seems that Basil was whole-hearted and consistent in his championship of cenobitism. In the monasteries under his control there is no sign that he allowed any passing over to a solitary life. When he became a bishop and was responsible for every department of Church life, he may have found it necessary to tolerate, and perhaps even further, varieties of monachism of which in the abstract he disapproved[2]. But the common life as described in his Rules was unaffected by this, and was handed down to later generations of Greek monks as the consistent working-out of a splendid, if unattainable, ideal.

ἔχουσα καλλιπυργώτους πόλεις. Cf. *Andr.* 1143. So far as it goes, this supports the interpreting of μιγάς in Gregory of the mingling of two opposites, i.e. the ascetic life and the world.

[1] On this and the following passages see Maran, *Vit. Bas.* IV. 4.

[2] *Hist. Laus.* XLV. 3, tells us how Basil was charmed with the austerity of Philoromus, who once shut himself up in a tomb for six years. Cf. Bas. *Ep.* 295.

# CHAPTER VII

## ST BASIL'S ASCETIC IDEALS

IF the reader has had the patience to work through the
material collected in the last chapter, he will have noticed
the richness and variety of thought with which Basil presents
his ascetic ideals, and the wide field over which his interests
range. Later legislators may have raised or lowered his
standards, or expressed with definiteness ideas that are only
implicit in his writings, but all the guiding principles of later
developments are already present in Basil, at least in germ[1].
The obligations have not often been expressed; the fact that
Basil composed no *rule* in the technical sense of the word has
detracted from his fame in the later Church. The average
monk during the ensuing centuries needed a set of definite clear-
cut rules, and Basil's instructions were not put in an attractive
or helpful form[2]. Their length was a serious drawback, and
it was not possible in practice to leave so much discretion
to the individual abbot as Basil had recommended. But, as

---

[1] Cf. Kranich, who ends his monograph with these words: "Nach Basilios
sind neue Ordensstifter aufgetreten, grosse, heilige Männer, deren Ruhm in alle
Welt gedrungen ist. Auch sie haben Anleitung zur Ascese gegeben, sie haben
Ordensregeln verfasst. Aber haben sie etwas wesentlich Neues, etwas wesentlich Anderes als Basilios ausgesprochen? Sie haben es nicht gethan, sie konnten
es nicht, sie durften es nicht." (*Die Ascetik in ihrer dogmatischen Grundlage bei
Basilios dem Grossen*, p. 97.)

[2] Cf. Meyer, *Die Haupturkunden*, p. 9, "Basilios...in seinen Anhängern mit
Leuten zu thun hatte, die von der ersten Begeisterung getragen, weniger eines
peinlichen Gesetzes als des weisen seelsorgerischen Raths bedurften, aber er
bildet auch den Grund, warum die Regeln des Basilios nicht die alleinige Grundlage für die Verfassung des griechischen Mönchtums werden konnten. Es
bedurfte vielmehr anderen Personlichkeiten, die den Idealen des grossen Kirchen-
vaters statutarische und disciplinelle Form gaben."

we shall presently see, his main principles passed into the common stock of monastic literature, both in East and West. The East revered him as the Father of its monasticism, though its actual guides have been other legislators who have not always been faithful to his ideals, while in the West his influence, mediated through the Benedictine Rule, has been wide-spread and lasting.

We have already sketched Basil's life as revealed in his letters and the orations of the two Gregories, and made a careful examination of his ascetic writings. It now remains to sum up the results of our investigation. The originality of the two sets of Rules, strongly attested by both external and internal evidence, seems quite indisputable to one who has studied the problem in all its bearings; so many are the coincidences between the Rules and Letters, and so strong is the general impression of an artistic unity. Had the Rules been composed even shortly after Basil's death, it would have been comparatively easy to detect signs of later date. The end of the fourth and beginning of the fifth century was a time of rapid change, and external events must inevitably have left their mark on the phraseology of documents[1].

We may accordingly assume the validity of the results already attained, and attempt to draw together the scattered threads of the investigation by sketching the broad outlines of Basil's work[2]. These may be considered under four heads.

I. The organisation of asceticism.
II. The moderation of existing austerities and enthusiasm.
III. The introduction of the common life.
IV. The bringing of monasticism into the service of the Church.

[1] The one serious objection to this statement of the unity of the picture is discussed in Additional Note B.

[2] I have confined my attention in the main to the practical aspects of the matter. The dogmatic presuppositions of Basil's asceticism have been worked out in admirable fashion by Kranich.

## I.   *The organisation of asceticism.*

Basil found the ascetic life firmly entrenched in Cappadocia and Pontus.   It took two forms.   First, the eremitic life lived in a cell by an individual; as in Egypt, so here in all probability this tended to pass into the semi-eremitic life, a number of ascetics living in more or less close neighbourhood and rendering voluntary deference to a senior. And, secondly, there was the later development of the traditional ascetic life in the world.   A number of persons— generally only two or three—lived a common life in one house; they were pledged to virginity, and devoted themselves to good works in the service of the Church.   But the ties thus formed were wholly voluntary and could be severed at any time.   The individual might feel himself bound by his own promise of virginity, but he was not obliged to maintain his relations with his fellow-ascetics.   Both the theory and practice of asceticism were unorganised[1].

Basil met the needs of the time with a clearly thought out system.   His views on marriage, judged by fourth century standards, were moderate, and he recognised its compatibility with goodness in the case of dwellers in the world[2].   But he made it perfectly plain that life in the world is lower *per se* than the life of asceticism.   The monk was in his eyes the Christian *par excellence*[3].   And so we find him urging the general adoption of the ascetic life.

Much of Basil's system was evidently of Egyptian origin. He had probably visited both Nitria and Tabennisi and witnessed the working of two different types of monasticism. He chose the Pachomian system as the model of his own institutions, but not without important alterations.   On returning to his native land, he was able to utilise the rising

[1] See pp. 45, 46.

[2] Gregory of Nyssa shows how it was possible to combine asceticism with sane views on marriage.   " Our view of marriage is this; that while the pursuit of heavenly things should be a man's first care, yet if he can use the advantages of marriage with sobriety and moderation, he need not despise this way of serving the State."   *De Virg.* 8.

[3] See F. 17.

enthusiasm for the ascetic life, and to found new monasteries, besides modifying the character of existing institutions. One of his objects was to have convents of moderate size, in contrast to the great numbers of monks found under the Pachomian regime. The Superior had many duties towards the individual monks which could only be discharged in a fairly small community. We read of "one lamp" and "one fire" sufficing for the whole brotherhood[1]. On the other hand, there is a tendency to exaggerate Basil's work in this direction and represent him as inaugurating a system of quite small monasteries. Everything points to the conclusion that his monasteries were of fair size, with perhaps 30 to 40 members. He advises the amalgamation of small communities in order to make one strong body, and the Rules depict a busy, self-centred community, large enough to supply its own wants, and requiring a number of officers.

The needs of women were not forgotten, but special care had to be exercised in their case, if the spread of monachism was not to result in scandal. The example of the Pachomian communities and Basil's own early experience showed the desirability of linking the two sexes. There were certain services that women could render to men, and they needed the help of the men for the administration of the Sacraments, the hearing of confessions, and general advice on the problems of government. Basil accordingly inaugurated a system of double monasteries, in which the abbot and abbess were in especially close connexion. The abbot ruled over the whole establishment, but his authority over the women was exercised through their head.

The different monasteries were joined in a kind of loose confederation. Periodical meetings of the Superiors were held, and the conflicting claims of the individual monastery and the confederation were met by a regulation that a new Superior was to be chosen by the Superiors of neighbouring monasteries, but the local monks must test and approve the choice. The general chapter of the Pachomian order was not reproduced, nor did anyone fill the place of the

[1] F. 35.

Superior-General in that system.    During Basil's life-time his
own personal ascendancy made such a device unnecessary.

We see then that Basil took over the general framework
of the Pachomian organisation, but modified it in the direction
of less strictness, leaving more scope for the voluntary action
of individuals.

II.    *The moderation of existing austerities and enthusiasm.*

Sulpitius Severus[1] uses some striking language on the
difference between the Gauls and the Egyptians.    A diet
that meant severe self-denial to the former seemed gluttony
to the latter.    The inhabitants of the high central plateau of
Asia Minor and the mountaineers of Pontus had constitutions
of the European rather than Egyptian type, and a modifi-
cation of physical austerities was desirable, if monasticism
was really to suit their needs.    Perhaps Basil had learned
a lesson from the effects of his own early privations.    At all
events, he fixed what he considered a reasonable standard of
austerity, and sternly forbade his monks to pass this limit.
No private fasts were allowed without the Superior's permission, and self-will was to be suppressed as much in this
as in any other direction.    Nothing corresponding to the
Egyptian custom of monks vying with one another in making
records in austerities was allowed in Basil's cenobia[2].

Basil's attitude towards "enthusiasm[3]" must be carefully
noted.. On the whole he limited it to small proportions.    The
general tone of the Basilian *Ascetica* comes as a surprise to a
student who is familiar with the Egyptian documents.    There
is a complete absence of the tales of miracles, clairvoyance,
spiritual healings, visions, and conflicts with demons, which

---

[1] *Dial.* I. 4, 8.

[2] Basil's moderation on this point must be judged, not by modern standards,
but by those of his own time.    See F. 17 for the thinness and paleness of the
Christian athlete.    The credit for the change of tone on this point must be
ascribed to Basil; moderation in fasting and penances was not a deduction drawn
of necessity by dwellers in an inclement climate, for the Irish hermits rivalled even
the Syrians in their austerities.    See *Camb. Med. Hist.* I. 534.

[3] I take the word from Holl's book *Enthusiasmus etc.*    Similarly in English
there is the technical (18th century) sense, of a consciousness of possessing special
gifts of the Spirit, such as aroused Bishop Butler's dislike.

play so large a part in the latter. The gifts of the Spirit for Basil mean moral and spiritual gifts rather than the power to see and do supernormal things. The last of the Longer Rules is most significant in this connexion; it deals at great length with the question of doctors and medicine, and vindicates their right to a place in the economy of the convent[1]. The modern reader will be inclined to give Basil considerable credit for this side of his work; it must be attributed in part to his common sense and his education, which had given him a thoroughly Greek sense of proportion. But the main cause was his diligent study of the New Testament and the extent to which he had appreciated the spirit of St Paul. He never attacks the conception of the miraculous which the revival of enthusiasm in Egypt had fostered, but he knows how to discriminate between the primary and secondary elements of religion[2].

Yet in one respect Basil adopted the new ideas, or rather revived ideas that had always been present in the Church, so that through him they obtained a permanent footing in Eastern monasticism. Although he was a bishop and magnified his office, he recognised that official rank does not always fit a man for the cure of souls; a special *charisma* of the Spirit was needed, which might be given in conjunction with the priesthood, but could also be possessed by a layman. There is nothing to show that a layman might not have held the highest offices in the monastery, and confession could be made to him, if he had the requisite spiritual gifts, as legitimately as to a priest.

### III. *The introduction of the common life.*

Of all the services rendered by Basil to the cause of monasticism, this is the one by which he most deserves to

---

[1] F. 55.

[2] Besse devotes Ch. XXIII. of *Les Moines d'Orient* to " Le merveilleux dans la vie des moines orientaux"; it contains no reference to Basil. Holl compares the relation of Basil to the Egyptian monks with that of St Paul to the popular conceptions of the early Church: "Basil had learned enough from Jesus and Paul to know what are in truth the highest gifts." In the Palestinian literature of the fifth century the miraculous reappears. *Op. cit.* pp. 166, 179—184.

be remembered. As we have already seen, the Pachomian monasteries were cenobitic only in outward appearance; their inner essence was individualist[1]. Basil made cenobitism a reality. Man was made for the common life, he declares, and not for the "monastic" life. The law of love, carried out in all its implications, forbids a solitary existence. This is the guiding principle of all Basil's regulations. The inculcation of a moderate standard of asceticism attainable by all was a natural deduction. So also was the practice of confession; since no man can live to himself, we need the help of one another in combating our sins. So also was the organisation of philanthropy, for the monastery must be so arranged as to give a practical outlet for the love of our neighbour[2].

## IV. *The bringing of monasticism into the service of the Church.*

If the introduction of the common life was the most important step taken by Basil in the strictly religious field, from the point of view of Church history it was even more significant that he welded into one the official Catholic Church and the new religious communities that were arising by its side and threatening to dissipate their energies in the desert. Basil is the first example of a man who was at once a great monk and a great bishop. The reconciliation took place first in his own person, and then through him in the Church at large. In his Rules he recognises here and there, if in a rather half-hearted way, the right of the bishop to be consulted in the affairs of the cloister, and in his own capacity as bishop he exercised a general superintendence over the monasteries of a wide area. He thus enlisted the services of monasticism to strengthen the Church, and, in so far as the Church of that day really served the State, monasticism also aided the State, instead of being, as is often supposed, its foe. In pursuance of his policy of bringing the monks

---

[1] p. 40.

[2] Basil did not advocate works of benevolence as an end in themselves, but as a necessary corollary of the love of God.

into relation with the episcopate Basil established cenobia in the towns instead of the desert. No longer was the monk to flee from his fellow-men, but by remaining in their midst to set them an example of a true Christian life[1].

The Basilian monasteries also served a useful purpose in providing education for children of both sexes. The primary aim was so to train the children that at a later age they might choose the monastic life as their own career. But no pressure was put upon them. The utmost care was to be taken to avoid unworthy professions; and the result must have been that many entered secular life after a training in the convent schools. If many men of the mental calibre of Basil were to be found in the monasteries, it was not surprising that parents left their children there to be educated. The curriculum was one-sided, worldly studies being excluded, but it may have been at least as good a training for life as the artificial "rhetoric" in vogue at the secular schools.

After this general sketch of the way in which Basil worked out his ascetic scheme, we may proceed to inquire what was the extent of his own contribution to monasticism. How much of his system was original, and how much derivative?

Now it is clear that Gregory helped his friend. But Gregory with all his genius was not a ruler of men, and the Rules with their breadth and sympathy evidently come from a man who was endowed to a marked degree with the gift of government; Gregory cannot have played more than a minor part in the composition of the Rules. To what extent the credit of Basil's work is really to be ascribed to Eustathius of Sebaste is an apparently insoluble problem, which need

---

[1] In spite of F. 6, which orders a remote situation for the monasteries, the above conclusion may be considered correct; Soz. *H.E.* VI. 17 and Cass. *Coll.* XVIII. 7 state clearly that Basil's monasteries were in the cities, and his later letters point the same way; probably the policy was not consciously adopted till his episcopate. Antony held that the desert was the monk's true home; out of it he perished, like a fish on dry land (Athan. *Vit. Ant.* 85; Soz. *H.E.* I. 13). Antony deferred even to a deacon (*Vit. Ant.* 67) but a different feeling towards Church officials was common in Egypt (Cass. *Inst.* XI. 17, omnimodis monachum fugere debere mulieres et episcopos). See Chrys. *de Sacerd.* VI. 6—8, for the inadequacy of the monastery as a school for bishops; cf. also Harnack, *History of Dogma*, III. 129.

only be alluded to here[1]. But the relation of Basil to
Pachomius is a question of considerable importance. Was
Basil really the "loyal disciple" of Pachomius, as he has
been styled[2]? It is clear that he made considerable use of
Pachomian ideas, but does the centre of gravity in his system
lie in those parts that were borrowed from Pachomius or in
his own original features?

An analysis of the sources of Basil's monastic system will
help us to an answer. They were three in number:

I.   The unorganised ascetic life which was found in Cappadocia and Pontus during Basil's childhood and youth, of
which such striking examples had existed in his own family
circle.

II.   The Rule of life practised in the Pachomian monasteries at the time of Basil's visit to Egypt in 358.

III.   The innovations which commended themselves to
his mature judgment as desirable in view of the needs of
the Church and the character of his fellow countrymen.

I.   The importance of this is twofold. In the first place,
the soil was already prepared when Basil began his work.
Everything was ready for a great religious revival, which,
as we saw in Chapter I, would necessarily take an ascetic
form. While it is best to be very cautious in assuming any
heathen influence upon Christianity, it is safe to assert that
the presuppositions of the native Anatolian religion had
produced a state of mind in the inhabitants of Cappadocia
that was favourable to the growth of monasticism[3]. And,
secondly, the influences which had played on Basil during
his childhood and youth had predisposed him in favour of
asceticism. After studying the attractive picture of the ascetic family life at Annesi, we shall not be disposed to think
it a mere coincidence that Basil's communities, unlike those of
Pachomius, were modelled on a family rather than a military
system.

[1] See Appendix A.    [2] By E. W. Watson, in *Ch. Quart. Rev.* Apr. 1907.
[3] See Ramsay in Hastings' *D.B.* v., art. "Religion of Greece and Asia
Minor." There seems to have been none of that genuine moral and intellectual
antipathy to asceticism which prevailed in the West in certain circles at a little
later period.

II. There is no sign that Basil drew any essential features of his system from Nitria or Scete, Palestine or Syria, or indeed from any foreign source except Tabennisi and its daughter houses. The resemblance between the Pachomian and Basilian Rules is very close in places, and descends at times even to minute details. For instance, the sections relating to the reception of slaves, the wearing of a girdle and of a distinct religious habit, the methods of manual work, the sale of the products of the workshops, the study of Scripture, the reception of visitors, and the relations between the two sides of the double monastery are very similar in the two Rules and sometimes almost verbally identical.

III. A number of points remain in which Basil is apparently under no obligations to Pachomius. He must be regarded as a pioneer in working out the ideal of the common life. Pachomius had the outward framework of a cenobium, but with Basil it became a living organism. The full implications of cenobitism were now realised for the first time. It was not to be a mere physical neighbourhood, a number of people obeying the same head, doing the same work and using the same church and refectory, but rather an idea bearing fruit in every department of life and spirit. Hence we have the cenobium depicted as the perfect mode of monachism; to leave it for the anchorite's cell is a retrogression. In keeping with this ideal private fasts and penances are forbidden, as mere ebullitions of self-will, and confession to a spiritual guide is inculcated as a religious necessity. Besides this fundamental principle of cenobitism there are other traits that show Basil's originality. The Superior is no military chief endowed with absolute power, but is subjected to certain limitations and checks. The elder brethren at least have the responsibility of judging his commands and testing them by the standard of the divine law. The monastery is not an *imperium in imperio*, a separate system by the side of or opposed to the official Church; it now becomes part of the Church, and recognises episcopal authority. Work was an important feature in the economy of Tabennisi, and so its place of honour in the Basilian monasteries need excite no remark. But the way in which the principle was worked out in Cappadocia was a novel and fruitful departure. The traditional philanthropy of the Church and the new monastic institutions now joined forces, and the latter became the agency through which the former worked. The great houses of charity and the convent schools for boys and girls are therefore another mark of Basil's originality. The Pachomian monastery was a busy hive of industry in which no drones were tolerated. The Basilian monastery was this and something more. Its energies were not confined within its own walls, but were consciously directed towards the alleviation of the sufferings of the outside world and the edification of the Church at large[1]. Finally, the Basilian system was based on Scripture. "It was possible," says Dr Harnack, "and in fact the danger was imminent, for the ascetic ideal to lose any assured connexion with Jesus Christ[2]." Such a criticism could hardly be levelled against Basil. No other monastic legislator has so wide a knowledge of the letter of the New Testament, or, in spite of some curiosities of interpretation, of its spirit as well. Christ's life of renunciation, His example and teaching, form the pattern after which Basil seeks to model his own instructions.

Thus Basilian monachism was composed of three strands, the first of comparatively slight importance. Of the two latter it is not difficult to see which was the more fundamental. Great as was the debt he owed to Pachomius, Basil's own contribution to monasticism was of greater weight and his ideas more potent. Dom Butler well remarks of the changes made by Basil: "The modifications are the result of the contact of the primitive ideas of monachism, as they existed in Egypt and the East, with European culture and modes of thought[3]."

Let us in conclusion try to expand these words. Up to

---

[1] Cf. Fialon, *Étude sur saint Basile*, p. 53, "Il fut le précurseur des François de Sales et des Vincent de Paul."

[2] *History of Dogma*, III. 131.     [3] *Lausiac History*, I. 244.

this point the development of monasticism had been in the hands mainly of Egyptian peasants; it was now directed by a man of high birth, a member of a family that had given a long line of officials to the government service. Basil was endued to the full with the spirit of the Empire; the Graeco-Roman power of organisation won in his monasteries yet another of its triumphs. Hitherto the leading monks had been either entirely ignorant, or else possessed of an education that compared unfavourably with that of many of their contemporaries outside the cloister. But "Basil was, as his name indicates, a true king among the spirits of his time[1]." In him the world saw with surprise the spectacle of one of the finest intellects of the age, educated at a great University and steeped in classical culture, offering his great attainments on the altar of the ascetic life[2]. The prestige that accrued to monachism must have been considerable, and the modifications of existing institutions made by a mind thus trained would be sure to make them more acceptable to Greek modes of thought. In Basil, too, monasticism and orthodoxy were identified. He and his followers were able to appreciate the bearings of abstruse theological controversies in a way that was impossible for their Egyptian predecessors, who were mentally less well equipped. And again; hitherto monasticism and the official Church had been, if not opposing, yet uncoordinated forces. In Basil the latent antagonism vanished, and the monks before long became the chief bulwark of the Byzantine Church.

Our next two chapters will show how far Basil's ideals were realised in later times. Some seem to have been too lofty, and perhaps not practical enough, to be generally comprehended. But if it is once granted that monasticism has a right to exist at all, no higher wish could be uttered on its behalf than that it should exemplify these three great

---

[1] Schäfer, *Basilius des Grossen Beziehungen zum Abendlande*, p. 205.

[2] According to Gregory of Nyssa Basil was the modern Moses, skilled in the wisdom of Egypt. *De Vit. Moy. P. G.* XLIV. 360. Cf. Puech, *St Jean Chrysostome*, p. 250 (quoted by Marin, *Les Moines de Constantinople*, p. 109), "L'ascétisme recrutait alors l'élite de la société chrétienne, comme dans les siècles précédents le christianisme avait recruté l'élite de la société païenne."

ideals that were Basil's contribution to its development—the earnest and consistent working out of the principle of the common life in all its implications, the offering up in its service of the highest secular culture of the time, and, as a logical consequence of its practice of the love of God, the manifestation of the love of man, especially in the alleviation of suffering and the education of the young.

# CHAPTER VIII

## SUBSEQUENT INFLUENCE IN THE EAST

OUR study of Basil from the point of view of monasticism is now complete. After trying in the opening chapters to investigate the sources of Basil's ideals, we proceeded to describe his activities in this field both before and during his episcopate, and discuss the problems connected with his ascetic writings. Before leaving the subject it will be well to indicate briefly what influence his conception of monachism has exercised upon the later Church. The natural division of the subject is into East and West, though, as will be seen in the next chapter, the existence of Greek monasteries in South Italy prevents the lines of demarcation from being quite clear.

What precisely is Basil's position to-day in the monastic traditions of the East? One answer frequently given is curiously far from the facts. The monks of the East, so it is said, belong to the Basilian Order[1]. The error is twofold. The Eastern monks are not Basilians, nor do they form an "Order" in the Western sense of the word. This is the conclusion of the best-informed among recent writers. Thus Dom Butler expresses himself in guarded terms: "To this

---

[1] Thus A. H. Hore, *Eighteen Centuries of the Orthodox Greek Church* (1899) speaks of the monasteries "following the Rule of St Basil" (p. 8) and of "the ancient unity of the Order of St Basil, which has subsisted ever since his time with its original simplicity" (p. 110). I. G. Smith, *Christian Monasticism*, p. 59, says "The Eastern monks preserved from the first with characteristic tenacity the Rule of Basil." Even Bardenhewer, *Patrologie* (1910), p. 245, says, "Die Basilianer sind der eine grosse Orden des Orients"; cf. Schneemann, *Kirchenlexicon*, art. "Basilianer," who describes them as "der grosse Orden der orientalischen Kirche."

day his (Basil's) reconstruction of the monastic life is the basis of the monasticism of the Greek and Slavonic Churches, though the monks do not call themselves Basilian[1]." A French writer who has travelled in the East is more uncompromising. The East, he says, has always shrunk from the idea of a grouping of monasteries into an Order. Rather does each individual convent form a distinct Order; only on Mount Athos do the peculiar local conditions present an approximation to an Order. Nor must the Byzantine monks be called Basilians. Eastern authors never use the term; they may speak of Akoimetes, Abrahamites, Studites, but never of Basilians. He has visited Saint-Sabbas, he continues, and found the monks most astonished that anyone should believe them related to Saint Basil; and the same sentiment was found prevailing on Mount Athos[2].

To check such a description would be impossible without a personal acquaintance with Eastern Church life. It is a simpler and perhaps more profitable task to ascertain how far the *spirit* of Basil has maintained itself in the East. Are his ideals still cherished in Oriental convents? If not, how and at what date did they lose their power? In order to answer these questions it will be necessary to give a brief summary of the post-Basilian development of Greek monachism; we shall then be in a better position to trace the persistence or disappearance of individual ideals.

The post-Basilian history may be divided for our purpose into four periods, each of which, owing to the presence of a great personality or for geographical reasons, has a unity of its own; from the point of time they overlap to some extent.

(i) The Palestinian period, during which the cenobitic and eremitic forms of monachism exist side by side.

---

[1] *Enc. Brit.* art. "Basilian Monks."

[2] Pargoire (in *Dict. d'archéol. chrét.* art. "Basile," col. 507, 508) puts the question, "Y a-t-il un ordre Basilien?" and answers it as above. Exception must however be taken to the following statement: "D'ailleurs, à part les congrégations égyptiennes des IVe et Ve siècles, l'Orient grec a toujours répugné à cette idée d'un groupement religieux qui réunirait ensemble plusieurs monastères." As shown above (p. 103) there are distinct traces in Basil's Rules of a grouping somewhat after the Pachomian model.

(ii) The early Constantinopolitan period, marked by the triumph of cenobitism, and the bringing of the monasteries under State control, a process which culminates in the legislation of Justinian.

(iii) The later Constantinopolitan period, characterised by the revival of cenobitism after a time of decay, the activity of Theodore, and the gradual acceptance of the Studium as reorganised by him as the normal type of monastery.

(iv) The later medieval and modern period, for which Mount Athos may be taken as typical.

(i) Basil's reputation was enhanced considerably by the triumph of Nicene orthodoxy at the Council of Constantinople in 381, but his monastic ideals spread but slowly. Sozomen ends his account of monasticism with a short paragraph on the monks of Cappadocia and the neighbouring provinces, in which he speaks as if their manner of life was peculiar to those countries[1]. Cenobitism naturally made most headway in the Churches under the influence of Caesarea, especially Pontus and Lesser Armenia[2]. The constant stream of pilgrims to the Holy Places brought Cappadocian ascetics to Palestine, and these helped to disseminate Basilian ideals. During the fifth and sixth centuries Palestine took the place in the history of monasticism that had been previously held by Egypt. Both forms of monasticism flourished on its soil, owing perhaps to its geographical situation between Cappadocia and Egypt, and the fact that it was a common meeting ground for different nationalities. Some of the more famous ascetics were Theodosius, Sabbas, Theognis, Euthymius and John the Silentiary, the first three of whom were Cappadocians[3]. A noticeable feature of the period is the way in which the adherents of the two systems lived side by side and cultivated the most friendly relations with one another. Theodosius was the head of the cenobites, and was styled

---

[1] *H.E.* vi. 34.

[2] Also in independent Armenia under the auspices of Narses. See Leclercq (*Dict. d'Archéol. chrét.* art. "Cénobitisme," col. 3142, 3).

[3] The main authority for this period is Cyril of Scythopolis, who wrote lives of the Palestinian monks. Our account is based on Holl, *Enthusiasmus*, pp. 171—191, and Meyer, *Die Haupturkunden*, pp. 10, 11.

L. C.

Archimandrite (or Exarch); the same title was also applied to Sabbas, the director of the eremites. Both classes of monks were subject to the authority of the patriarch of Jerusalem, and there were even times when all the ascetics had one and the same head[1]. It was not unknown for a laura (a complex of anchorites' cells) to become a cenobium. Thus Euthymius had a dream bidding him form his monks into a cenobium, since that mode was more pleasing to God[2]. But the general tendency was the other way. The cenobium was regarded in the light of a school in which a monk could prepare himself for complete retirement. So for a young man at least the cenobium was the right place[3], and it was not safe to contend against the evil spirits which attacked the solitary without a careful preliminary training[4]. But solitude was considered the higher life; to leave the cloister for the cell was to go "from glory to glory[5]." Sabbas the head of the anchorites once said to Theodosius the head of the cenobites: "My lord abbot, you are a Superior of children, but I am a Superior of Superiors, for each of those under me is independent and therefore Superior of his own cell," and Theodosius received the pleasantry with approval[6].

All this is very far removed from Basil's ideal of the common life. The stronger spirits aimed at an unbroken communion with God, and the petty details of convent life distracted them from their purpose. Holl pertinently asks[7] whether Basil could have lived in one of his own cenobia; he points out also that there were special difficulties in Palestine to prevent the realisation of the cenobitic ideal, in that it was the duty of the monasteries to offer hospitality to the pilgrims who came in such numbers. But Basil's conception was undoubtedly the higher, at least from a modern

[1] Holl, p. 173.
[2] *Vita Euthymii*, pp. 30, 80, 88; cf. Holl, p. 174.
[3] *Vita Euthymii*, p. 68; Holl, p. 175.
[4] Theod. *vita Theodosii*, p. 12; Holl, *ib.*
[5] *Vita Theodosii*, p. 14; Holl, *ib.*
[6] *Vita Sabbae*, p. 332 C; Holl, *ib.* See also Meyer, p. 10; the celliote is to be διδακτικόν, οὐ χρῄζοντα διδασκαλίας.
[7] p. 176.

standpoint, and Palestinian monachism represented a declension from his ideal. With the Arabian invasions the importance of Palestine waned, but the miseries of the time made men more than ever inclined to embrace a life of asceticism. Under such circumstances it was natural that the less organised form should prove more attractive, and indeed it was better fitted to survive.

(ii) Constantinople, the new capital of the Empire, soon became the main centre of Greek monachism, with important consequences for the future of the movement[1]. For at the capital the State was naturally all-powerful, and it proved impossible for monasticism to resist the determination of the Byzantine Emperors to bring every department of life under their control; for a time at least it fell a victim to their centralising policy. Our knowledge of Byzantine monachism is imperfect and the background to the ascetic literature remains obscure[2]. It seems best therefore to take one central figure as typifying the tendencies of a whole period, and ignore secondary persons and movements. For the early Constantinopolitan period Justinian is clearly the dominant influence.

The convent life of the capital in its early stages resembled that of other localities, except in so far as imperial influence played a part from the first[3]. A new and unwelcome feature of ascetic life was displayed in the city during the great doctrinal controversies, when large numbers of monks flocked thither from the provinces, rousing general resentment by their turbulent lawlessness. The Council of Chalcedon tried to check these vagrants by putting all monasteries under the control of the bishop of the diocese, and forbidding the occupants to leave the cloister or take part in external

[1] For this section see Holl and Meyer as before; also Marin, *Les Moines de Constantinople*, who gives an exhaustive account, but is apt to draw a composite picture without distinguishing sufficiently the sources from which the details are derived.

[2] So Ehrhard in Krumbacher's *Geschichte der byzantinischen Litteratur*, C. 139. " Unsere Kenntnis von den konkreten Zuständen in der byzantinischen Klosterwelt ist nun leider noch zu lückenhaft, um den historischen Hintergrund, von dem sich die ganze Litteraturgattung abhebt, genau erkennen zu können."

[3] See Marin, *Les Moines de Constantinople*, pp. 4, 44.

affairs without his permission[1]. Monastic discipline was
sharpened still further by Justinian. Like other Byzantine
ecclesiastical legislators, he did not consider himself an
innovator, but claimed to follow the tradition of "the holy
fathers," and codify existing regulations. In his legislation
he insisted on a common life, making it the one legal form
of monachism, and forbidding any monk to have his private
dwelling or "cell" (τὸ λαλούμενον κέλλιον). This rule however allowed of some exceptions. Those who wished to live
a life of contemplation might have anchorites' cells, *but inside
the cenobium*; the number of such was to be strictly limited[2].
Either this legislation was only intended for the cenobia
—the anchorites being omitted as relatively unimportant—or
else it proved abortive, for in the next period we find
solitaries clustered round a famous ascetic, just as they had
done from the beginning[3].

Justinian also strengthened the power of the bishop, who
was to preside over the founding of a monastery by fixing
a cross[4], conduct the election of a new abbot by the monks,
and exercise a general legal as well as ecclesiastical jurisdiction over them[5]. A probation of three years was fixed,
during which secular clothing was worn. After this the
monk was professed and received the religious habit (σχῆμα)[6].
Several of the older monks were to be ordained in order to
take the services, but if there was no church in the monastery,
the monks went to the nearest church, returning immediately
after the service[7]. They were tied down to their monastery,
and could only go out with the abbot's consent[8]. Double
monasteries were forbidden[9].

---

[1] Can. 4; cf. 8.
[2] *Nov.* 5, 3; 133, *praef.* 1.
[3] See Meyer, pp. 11—14 and Holl's criticism, pp. 193—6. The latter says,
"Meiner Meinung nach ist also von den freien Anachoreten und von Lauren
in der ganzen Gesetzgebung Justinian's überhaupt nicht die Rede. Justinian
kümmert sich nur um die κοινόβια und will, dass dort der κοινὸς βίος wirklich
durchgeführt werde." On p. 197 he gives instances of the old type of laura in the
following centuries.
[4] σταυροπηγία. A wooden cross was buried behind the high altar.
[5] *Nov.* 5, 1; 131, 7; 133, 4.
[6] *ib.* 123, 35.
[7] *ib.* 133, 2.
[8] *ib.* 133, 1.
[9] *ib.* 123, 36.

The general tendency of this is clear. Organised monasticism as found in the cenobia was to be subject to the bishops, and through them to the State. Unorganised asceticism was of less importance and could be left out of view. To outward appearance Basil's cenobitic system conquered, but the inner spirit evaporated. The anchorite ideal gained a firm footing within the cenobia, and under the circumstances it was easy and natural to regard it as the higher mode of life.

(iii) The Byzantine State Church continued to exercise a controlling influence over the internal affairs of monasticism. The Trullan Council in 692 forbade any monk to become an eremite without a three years' probation in a cenobium[1]. A desire was felt by many monasteries to get rid of the control of the diocesan bishop and come directly under the patriarch. Germanus (715—730) furthered this movement, which was prompted by the same motives as the similar tendency in the West, by ordering that all monasteries at whose foundation the patriarchal cross had been used should remain within the patriarch's jurisdiction[2]. By this time the ideas of the so-called Dionysius the Areopagite had become a force in Greek monachism, and the priestly and monastic ranks were accordingly thought of as " mysteries," deserving of equal honour and corresponding to the vocations of Martha and Mary respectively[3].

We now reach Theodore of Studium, the greatest figure, after Basil, in the history of Greek-speaking monachism[4]. About 463 Studius, an ex-consul, had founded a church at Constantinople which was called the Studium after its founder. Though not intended originally for their use, it was occupied before long by the Akoimetai ("Sleepless Ones"), a body of monks founded by Alexander (died c. 430). Their distinguishing characteristic was the maintenance of an unceasing round of prayer and praise. The monastery reached a great size, and the members were divided into "choruses" for the purposes of devotion. Towards the end of the eighth century

[1] Can. 41.    [2] Zöckler, *Askese und Mönchtum*, p. 294.
[3] Zöckler, p. 292.
[4] To the authorities already cited add Miss A. Gardner, *Theodore of Studium*.

this monastery had fallen from its high estate, and its numbers had dwindled to ten[1]. Theodore was the means of its revival and reorganisation. Born of a noble family in 759, he had renounced the world in company with other members of his family, and had received his early lessons in asceticism from his uncle Paul, the abbot of Saccudio. Paul formed the highest opinion of his nephew and promoted him to be abbot in his place. As Theodore would not let his uncle retire, the two ruled for a while as joint-abbots, first at Saccudio, and then at Studium (789). The time was ripe for a revival in monasticism, which had fallen on evil days, partly perhaps because its free spirit had been crushed by an excess of State regulation. But the Church now came to realise that it was more than a mere department of State, and put forth its whole strength in the struggle against the iconoclast Emperors. Monasticism had to bear the brunt of the battle; while the parish priests submitted to the imperial orders, the convents resisted and had in consequence to endure cruel persecutions. But, when the final victory was won, monasticism enjoyed a renewed life and increased prestige.

Theodore's main inspiration came from a study of the monastic fathers, and especially the ascetic works of Basil[2]. He revived the common life, and insisted on the carrying out of the obligations of brotherhood even to the minutest details, such as a common stock of clothes. The abbot's powers were increased, and under him was placed a row of other officials who were obliged to report to him everything that happened. Constant instruction of the brethren in the principles of asceticism and their application to community life was made a special feature of the system. Provision was made for education and the care of the sick, but "the sick, as the young, seem to have been members of the community." A certain amount of philanthropic work, such as doles to the poor, visiting of invalids and prisoners, and performing of funeral rites, was also undertaken by the monks[3].

---

[1] Gardner, p. 67.

[2] Cf. Ehrhard (in Krumbacher), p. 147, "Massgebende Autorität für das geistliche Leben ist für ihn Basilios, nicht der Pseudoareopagite."

[3] Gardner, pp. 71—79.

A point of some interest may be mentioned here. Theodore deprecates the custom of giving two different habits, the Little and the Great: " Do not give what they call the little habit, and then, some time later, another as the larger. For there is one habit, as there is one baptism, and this is the practice of the Holy Fathers. Depart not from the rules and canons of the Fathers, especially of the holy Father Basil[1]." The purpose of the arrangement was to set some of the brethren free for the contemplative life. To the monks of the Little Habit fell the practical work of the monastery, such as the entertainment of visitors ; the abbot, as the business head of the community, was chosen from their number[2]. The origin of the distinction is obscure, but it was clearly connected with the custom, provided for in Justinian's Laws, of allowing some of the monks to pass from the cenobitic to the eremitic or higher stage. In protesting against it Theodore proved himself a true son of Basil.

The reformed convent of Studium became a centre from which influences streamed out to all parts of the Greek world. Many parts of Theodore's Rules were adopted on Mount Athos, which in its turn became the headquarters of monasticism. Moreover, the monastery of Kief in South Russia drew its inspiration from Studium, and so through Kief Studium has affected the whole of the later ecclesiastical history of Russia[3].

The later Constantinopolitan period is marked therefore by a revival of Basilian ideas. In so far as Basil only adumbrated principles which were not thoroughly worked out till Theodore's time, the latter may be called the true legislator of Greek cenobitism. But we must remember that the monasteries were not all Studite, even after Theodore's influence had spread far and wide. Lauras of semi-eremitic

---

[1] Gardner, p. 73 (Migne, *P. G.* XCIX. 1820 C). This is the earliest mention of the distinction, τὸ μικρὸν σχῆμα and τὸ μέγα σχῆμα.

[2] Holl, pp. 200—202. Butler (*Enc. Brit.* art. "Basilian Monks") compares the distinction in the West between choir-monks and lay-brothers. But the practice of choosing the abbot from the possessors of the Little Habit seems to make the comparison of little value. Both grades were of course and still are quite independent of sacerdotal rank.

[3] Meyer, p. 19.

monks, such as we found in early times and shall meet again in the next period, did not cease to exist. And certain changes had been made in the common life as understood by Basil, for a custom had grown up, so Theodore tells us, of allowing some of the monks to withdraw from the common life and apply themselves exclusively to contemplation; they wore a distinctive robe and without doubt enjoyed a higher estimation.

(iv) For the latest period of Greek monachism we are justified in confining ourselves to Mount Athos[1], which in this respect is a microcosm of the Eastern Church. " The Holy Mountain" has been the chief sanctuary of Eastern asceticism for nearly a thousand years. " He who knows the history of the convents of the Holy Mountain, knows the history of Greek monasticism in its completest form[2]."

The beginnings of the movement followed the same course as elsewhere. First of all, in the ninth century, there were solitaries; Peter the Athonite landed on the peninsula about 840, and is said to have lived in a cave for fifty years, while Euthymius of Thessalonica, another famous pioneer, arrived in 859[3]. Then came a loose grouping of solitaries, and finally the fully developed monasteries. The chief law-giver during these early days was Athanasius, who lived in the latter half of the tenth century. His leading ideas were derived from the Studium, and so ultimately from Basil. He allowed five anchorites within the cenobium or laura[4], but, a somewhat unusual trait, considered theirs a lower vocation than that of those who remained in the common life[5]. These early convents belonged to a class which had grown up during the preceding period, but of whose origin there is no clear trace; they were independent, and outside the jurisdiction of the Church authorities. However, in 1312 the reigning Emperor rectified this anomaly by putting the

[1] Besides Meyer, Lake, *The Early Days of Monasticism on Mount Athos* and Riley, *Athos, or The Mountain of the Monks* are useful. Cf. Curzon, *Visits to Monasteries of the Levant.*

[2] Meyer, p. 4.          [3] Lake, pp. 12, 41—52.

[4] We now find *laura* used in this new sense, as equivalent to cenobium.

[5] Meyer, p. 28. These anchorites are now called Celliotes.

Protos (general superintendent of the Holy Mountain) under the patriarch of Constantinople and ordering him to receive his consecration from the latter[1].

In the later middle ages a new and surprising development took place, namely, the rise of the idiorrhythmic system. Under this arrangement the monks retained their private property, the Protos disappeared, and the organisation of the community assumed a loosely democratic form. The first trace of the new system appears in 1374, but the time of its greatest prosperity, both in Athos and elsewhere, was the sixteenth century. It must not be taken as implying a return to the eremitic ideal, for the eremitic system continued to have its place by the side of the idiorrhythmic monasteries, but rather as superseding the cenobia[2]. The sixteenth century was marked by a decay of zeal, to which both the political situation and the idiorrhythmic system contributed. From that time onward a steady improvement has been witnessed. In the eighteenth century a reaction in favour of cenobitism set in, and has continued. The Skitae also received their constitution at this time, though they had existed since the sixteenth century. These are anchorites living at a distance from a monastery, but reckoned as members of it. They lead a life of considerable austerity, and most of the Great Habit monks are now found among their number. They are to be distinguished carefully from the modern Celliotai, on whom no special ascetic obligation is laid, and who are really solitary monkish peasants[3].

At the present time all three types of monachism—the eremitic, cenobitic and idiorrhythmic—are represented on Mount Athos and in the Eastern Church generally. The official Church however has remained true to early ideals and mistrusts the idiorrhythmic type as a secularised form of monasticism. But, if we may judge from Mr A. Riley's words,

[1] Meyer, pp. 25, 54.

[2] Meyer, pp. 57 ff. Cf, p. 2 for the ultimate significance of the movement, "Mit dem Eigenthum findet auch die Cultur ihren Weg in das Kloster. Luxus und Weltleben sind eingedrungen, aber auch Interesse für Bildung und Wissenschaft, für die Aufgaben der Cultur, für die Nationalität."

[3] Meyer, pp. 71, 83—86.

the system is in closer touch with modern ideas than its rivals. "In an idiorrhythmic monastery each monk lives as he pleases; if rich he has a suite of apartments, if poor he shares a cell with a brother. Discipline is kept up by public opinion rather than by authority....We were much surprised at hearing that the idiorrhythmic system was the more economical of the two (i.e. the idiorrhythmic and cenobitic). The monks explained that in this case each inmate cultivated his own little garden, and we were led to infer that when they worked for themselves individually they accomplished more than when they laboured for the common weal[1]." Meyer also points out that this type has been more in touch with the reviving spirit of Nationalism than the others, and may well have an important part to play in the future[2]. The cenobitic type persists; these monks are still governed by an abbot (*hegoumenos*) and preserve the distinction of novices, the Little Habit, and the Great Habit. Of the latter it is reported that "very few enter this, the highest monastic grade, which entails almost complete withdrawal from earthly things and a life entirely devoted to religious exercises. The great majority of the Athos monks belong to the second grade, of the Little Habit, though many assume the Great Habit on their death-beds[3]." The common life, that is to say, survives, but to withdraw from it as far as possible is the monk's highest ideal. And, finally, just as eremitism was the earliest form of monachism, so in a sense it is the latest, for throughout the East this type still exists in much of its pristine vigour.

The national jealousies which have been the bane of Eastern Christendom are reproduced in the monasteries, which keep closely to the lines of nationality[4]. In other respects as well the Western observer will find material for

---

[1] *Athos*, pp. 66, 378, 379.       [2] pp. 2, 3, 60.

[3] Riley, *Athos*, p. 68.

[4] Meyer, p. 89, "Das russische Mönchtum ist ein anderes als das griechische, das rumänische ein anderes als das bulgarische oder serbische. Russen, Griechen, Rumänen könnten heute nur mit gewalt in einem und demselben Kloster dauernd zusammengehalten werden. Ein gemeinsames Leben in Frieden und Liebe gäbe das nicht."

unfavourable criticism in the monasteries of the East. It would be surprising if they did not show scars of conflict from the secular struggle with the Turk. But, much as Greek-speaking monachism has suffered from this cause, it is doubtful whether the course of development would have been much different, even if the Byzantine Empire had stood to this day. Russia is the true heir to the spiritual kingdom of Constantinople, and Russian monasticism in all essentials is one with that of the Greek-speaking Church.

The foregoing sketch of 1500 years of Greek monastic life, in spite of its inadequacy, may perhaps serve a purpose in providing a historical framework for our account of Basil's influence on the later Church. Let us now inquire how far first his actual Rules, then the ideals enshrined in them, have maintained their position in Eastern monasticism.

Basil's Rules have always held a high place in the theory of the Eastern Church. During the Palestinian period they formed a subject of instruction in the convents[1]. When Justinian and other legislators spoke of "the holy fathers," they had Basil chiefly in mind. Theodore of Studium embodied much of their contents in his own Constitutions. Studium had, so to speak, daughter-houses at Kief and on Mount Athos, and Athanasius specially recommended the study of Basil's works to the monks of Athos[2]. But there must always have been many who were ready to cry with the twelfth century abbot, What need have we of such writings[3]? At the present time, so Mr Riley says, " Oriental monks are not governed by any code of laws laid down by any particular saint or founder, but are bound by the *Canons*, i.e. the monastic disciplinary enactments of the Oecumenical Councils of the Catholic Church, especially of that part of the Sixth Council known as the Concilium in Trullo[4]." Dom Butler puts the matter rather differently : " To this day the Rules of Basil and the Constitutions of Theodore the

---

[1] Holl, p. 173.    [2] See Meyer, p. 18.

[3] Referring to Gregory of Nazianzus. Euthymius of Thessalonica reports the incident, see Ehrhard in Krumbacher, *Geschichte der byzantinischen Litteratur*, C. 140.

[4] *Athos*, p. 65.

Studite, along with the Canons of the Councils, constitute the chief part of Greek and Russian monastic law[1]." There is an apparent difference of opinion between the two writers, but only on the surface. The monasteries, so it seems, have a general body of disciplinary regulations which are held in theoretical honour and among which the Rules of Basil are the oldest and perhaps most famous, but each convent is more or less a law to itself, and its own tradition and public opinion are far more important than would be the case in the West. In actual practice the Basilian Rules are very little known or studied.

But have not the monks of the East perhaps remained faithful to the tradition of Basil, even while they have known little of his Rules? To go through the Rules in detail and show to what extent they were repeated in later Canons and Constitutions would be a formidable task and quite outside the limits of the present study[2]. It may be readily granted that some of Basil's regulations have been repeated by later legislators and have passed into the common stock of Eastern Church custom. But when we look below the surface it will be seen that the distinctive principles of Basil's ascetic work have not been the dominating influences in Greek monasticism. It has been shown above[3] that Basil's main contribution to monasticism lay in his advocacy of the common life as the highest type of asceticism, from which he drew certain logical consequences, such as the observance of a moderate standard of austerity attainable by all, and the necessity of frequent confession. Hardly less important than this was the extent to which he brought the monasteries into close relations with the official Church as represented by the episcopate, and the practical activities by which the monks were to serve the Church and humanity at large. A service less conspicuous, but not to be left out of consideration, was his consecration of the highest culture of the day on the altar of the ascetic life.

---

[1] *Enc. Brit.* art. "Basilian Monks."

[2] A good deal of material will be found in Marin, *Les Moines de Constantinople.*

[3] See pp. 123—126.

It may be said at once without fear of contradiction that on the most crucial point of all the later Church has never assimilated Basil's teaching. Cenobitism has endured through the centuries as a possible mode of monachism. For much of the time it has shared the field with the eremitic system; during the last 500 years, since the rise of idiorrhythmic monasteries, it has been only one out of three possible systems. Not only has Basil's cenobitism failed to establish itself as the prevailing method, but even within the cenobium itself the common life as understood by him has received a fatal blow in the intrusion of the solitary life. Even Justinian, who attempted to make the cenobitic the normal form of monachism, by allowing solitaries within the cenobium made it clear that he regarded the eremitic life as the higher. The tendency finally crystallised into the institution of the Great Habit, the possessors of which are considered by public opinion to have chosen the better part[1]. The austerities of later Greek monachism have not as a rule been excessive; but it would be better to attribute this to a natural declension from the rigour of early ideals than to any consistent working-out of the consequences of the common life, such as is found in Basil's Rules.

The alliance between the secular Church and monasticism inaugurated by Basil has proved permanent[2]. It has even become an organic union, since it is the common custom for the episcopate to be recruited from the monasteries, while the married parish priests are debarred from the highest order of the Church. This has probably operated in two ways; it has certainly caused asceticism to be recognised as the highest form of Christianity, but the chief officers of the Church, as might be expected from their training, have been on the whole markedly deficient in knowledge of affairs and powers of leadership. Except in the case of convents under the influence of Studium, Eastern monachism has not in the later centuries preserved the Basilian traditions in the matter of

---

[1] Justinian (*Nov.* 5, c. 3) describes those who lived in the cells as τῆς κοινότητος ἐπὶ τὸ κρεῖττον ἐξῃρημένους.

[2] Athos has been in some respects an exception to the rule.

the care of the sick and the education of the young. The neglect of practical activities in favour of an exclusive effort after the contemplation of God is a natural consequence of the weakening of the cenobitic ideal.

In the intellectual field Byzantine monachism rendered no mean service in the early middle ages by its literary labours[1]. But at the present time the Eastern monks, with a few honourable exceptions, are quite out of touch with the intellectual movements of the age, and their neglect of the literary treasures of which they are custodians is the despair of European *savants*.

It would seem then that the characteristically Basilian features of monasticism have made but little appeal to the mind of the later Greek Church. Nor is the case otherwise if we consider certain principles which Basil did not originate, but took over from Pachomius and recommended for general adoption, such as manual labour, the grouping of monasteries into a kind of order or federation, and the close association of the two sexes. The element of continuous hard work as an essential factor in monastic life has been practically eliminated from the Eastern monasteries of to-day. Basil wished the monks of higher education to apply themselves mainly to mental labour and sacred study ; but the putting of manual labour into the background has not been accompanied by any compensating emphasis on theological studies. Eastern monachism has always remained to a great extent formless. The maxim "Union is Strength" has never been appreciated, and Basil's plans for linking the monasteries of a district, and calling periodical conferences of abbots, have never been properly carried out[2]. And again, the institution of double monasteries belonged to a time of primitive enthusiasm.

[1] See Ehrhard in Krumbacher, *op. cit.* p. 140, "Die byzantinischen Mönche stehen nicht nur in der ersten Reihe der theologischen Schriftsteller ; ohne sie würde auch die Zahl der profanen Litteraten nicht unwesentlich zusammenschrumpfen ; namentlich wenn man beachtet dass viele derselben erst dann Zeit und Lust zu litterarischen Schaffen fanden, als sie sich in ein Kloster zurückgezogen hatten."

[2] There was however some such organisation in Constantinople and its neighbourhood, where the term Archimandrite was used for the Superior of a group of monasteries.

It proved unworkable and was definitely forbidden by Justinian. One can sympathise with the reaction from pagan license which caused so strong a movement towards personal purity and made even Basil's double monasteries an object of suspicion, in spite of the numerous safeguards which he devised. But ordinances such as that which excludes even female animals from the precincts of a convent of men cannot but strike the observer as ridiculous.

In writing the above we have not wished to disparage the medieval and modern developments of Greek monachism—to seek God by a process of abstraction from phenomena is as legitimate as the method, more popular in modern times, of seeking Him in phenomena—only to point out that, as a matter of history, Basil's ideals have not been realised in the East. He was in many ways of a thoroughly Western temperament, active, restless, and full of organising and ruling ability. It is not surprising if the East, while revering his name, has misunderstood his spirit[1].

These then are the results of our investigation. Basil's Rules form part of the traditional authorities on which the monks of the East rely. Some of their details have passed into the common stock of tradition, and are still practised to-day. But there is no Basilian Order ; the modern monks do not call themselves by Basil's name. Nor should it be applied to them by outsiders, for in many important respects they observe neither the letter nor the spirit of his ascetic writings.

---

[1] In the political and economic spheres the Christian nations of the Near East have now entered into the family of European nations. But in ecclesiastical matters the traditional distinction between the spirit of the West and that of the East seems still valid.

# CHAPTER IX

## SUBSEQUENT INFLUENCE IN THE WEST

BEFORE deciding to what extent Basil's influence in the East was permanent, we found it necessary to sketch the fortunes of Greek monachism down to the present day. The question of his influence in the West is not less important, but in this case the inquiry can be confined within narrower limits and need not extend beyond Benedict. Any influence that the Rules of Basil may have had on the later Western Church has been indirect, and mediated through the Benedictine Rule.

There is a subsidiary question that should be discussed before attacking the main problem, namely, the Greek monasteries of South Italy and Sicily. These form an interesting by-path of Church History, but are of no real significance for the history of monasticism, though they form a link of some importance in the development of European culture. They were in reality a piece of Eastern Church life transplanted to the West, which gradually yielded to the influences of its environment and became thoroughly Westernised. Here at last we shall find what we failed to find in the East, a " Basilian Order " in a true sense[1].

The southernmost provinces of Italy, Calabria and Apulia, after suffering severely in the Lombard invasions, became almost completely Hellenised in the following centuries, and remained part of the Byzantine Empire until they were

---

[1] The following account is drawn mainly from some valuable articles by Prof. Lake in the *Journal of Theological Studies* (1902, 1903), with help from Schneemann (art. " Basilianer " in *Kirchenlexicon*), Pargoire (art. " Basile" in *Dict. d'Archéol. chrét.*) and Heimbucher, *Die Orden*, pp. 46, 47.

conquered by the Normans in the middle of the eleventh
century. Sicily was conquered from the Greeks by the
Saracens at an earlier period (827—902). The political
situation was reflected in the ecclesiastical world, and for a
long period the Church in Sicily and South Italy was an
integral part of the patriarchate of Constantinople. During
the seventh century a stream of settlers came from the East
to these Western provinces, many of them fleeing from the
troubles which were devastating the Levant. A large number
of monks came with the settlers, some of whom went to
Rome and other Latin centres, where, though preserving for
a while the Greek language and manner of life, they were
soon assimilated in all essentials to the neighbouring Latin
monasteries. Others went to Sicily and kept their Greek
character. South Italy was almost a desert at this time, and
may be left out of consideration. Its importance began in
the ninth century, when the Greeks fled across the straits of
Messina to escape from the Saracen invasions of Sicily.
The beginnings of monachism here followed the same course
of development as elsewhere among the Greeks—first solitary
ascetics, then a period of lauras, then true cenobitic convents. There is no trace of the existence of any Basilian[1]
monasteries in Calabria before 850 or thereabouts. Owing
to the Saracen raids, which exercised a continuous pressure
from the south, there was a tendency to move northwards.
Before long the monks showed signs of greater union among
themselves, and a desire to cultivate literary studies. When
the Normans came, they found a great number of Basilian
monasteries, using the Greek language and strongly opposed
to Rome. In pursuance of their policy of reducing ecclesiastical affairs to order, they Latinised many of the
monasteries, which now passed under the Benedictine Rule.
But in purely Greek districts the Basilian convents were
allowed to remain; in fact new ones were founded and the

---

[1] The word is convenient, though in their origin these monasteries were no
more Basilian than the corresponding ones of the East. They became Basilian in
course of time; the existence of neighbouring convents owning Benedict as a
spiritual father probably led them to emphasise their relation to the father of
Greek monachism.

L. C.                                                                          10

old monasteries placed under their control, a method which was found better suited to the requirements of the feudal system.    But the tendency to Latinisation proved irresistible, and set in strongly during the thirteenth century, when the Greeks were practically Romanised.    In the fifteenth century the individuality of these convents was temporarily revived. They now became a fully-developed Order in the Western sense.    There was great enthusiasm at the time for Hellenic studies, and hopes of a reunion between East and West were entertained.  In 1446 a general council of the Order of St Basil was held, and Bessarion was appointed General of the Order; he made a *résumé* of the Basilian Rules, which was to be the formal Rule of the Order.    He was also a great collector of manuscripts, and it is important to notice that, when the revival of interest in Greek literature began in Italy, there was a number of traditional Greek centres near to hand in these monasteries, many of which had valuable libraries.

This intensification of the Greek side of the Basilian convents was only temporary, and before long they became completely absorbed in the Roman Church.    A brief sketch of their subsequent history may be not without interest.

In 1573 Gregory XIII instituted a further reform, making them into a centralised congregation, in which certain Spanish Basilians were included.    At the present time very few traces of the Order remain in the West.    The famous monastery of Grotta Ferrata (founded in 1002 by St Nilus) still exists, and is treated by the Italian Government as a historical monument ; the Greek rite is still used within its walls.    There is another in Toronto, the daughter-house of a small French convent at Annay.    A number of monasteries are to be found among the Ruthenians, who were united to the Roman Church in 1596, mainly through the influence of the Basilians. Pius VII in 1822 described them as "the great support of the true faith among the Ruthenians."    There are also a few Basilian monasteries among the Uniat bodies of the East, and in this way the Basilians have returned to their original home, having assumed at last, thanks to the organising spirit of the West, the form of a true " Order."

We must now return to the main stream of Church life and trace the influence of Basil's Rules on Latin-speaking monachism[1]. An unorganised ascetic life had been known in Italy from an early date, though it had not been practised so widely as in the East. But the monastic life proper was introduced in the West at a definite time, and struck the imagination of the Italians as something novel[2]. The visit of Athanasius to Rome in 339 accompanied by two Eastern monks may be considered the historical origin of Western monachism. Through him, either now or a little later, the story of Antony's life was introduced to the knowledge of the West and became the recognised model for monks. Monasteries of the Antonian type were rapidly organised, amongst which the most famous are Ambrose's foundation at Milan, and the convent at Aquileia where Rufinus and Jerome received their training in the ascetic life. In France the first great popular figure in the records of monachism was the famous Martin of Tours, whose monastery outside the city "was a simple reproduction of the Antonian monachism of Egypt[3]." These early Western monks were felt to be no whit inferior to the Easterns, and the fame of Martin spread all over the East soon after his death[4]. Monasticism throughout the world was conscious of a fundamental spiritual unity.

At the end of the fourth century other influences began to assert themselves. In 397 Rufinus returned to Aquileia after his travels in the East, and at the request of Urseius, abbot of Pinetum, translated the Rules of Basil into Latin. He interpreted his task with some freedom, and out of the original 55 Longer and 313 Shorter Rules made a new edition of 203 Rules[5]. This version was the channel through

---

[1] Spreitzenhofer, *Die Entwicklung des alten Mönchtums in Italien* is the fullest description of the pre-Benedictine period.

[2] See p. 31.

[3] Butler, *Lausiac History*, I. 245. Jerome, *Ep.* 58, shows how the Egyptian anchorites were the recognised model: "Romani duces imitentur Camillos, etc.... Nos autem habeamus propositi nostri principes Paulos et Antonios, Julianos, Hilariones, Macarios."

[4] Sulp. Sev. *Dial.* I. 23—26.          [5] See Appendix B.

which the Basilian system reached the West. Rufinus shows in his preface that he anticipated its use in many convents. But pre-Benedictine Western monasticism was eclectic in its methods and there is no sign that any community adopted the Basilian Rules just as they stood. They were only one among many forces that influenced the West. No doubt the reputation of Ambrose had something to do with their favourable reception. Ambrose was a great admirer of Basil, and in compiling his *Hexaemeron* made considerable use of Basil's work on the same subject. Dionysius, Ambrose's (orthodox) predecessor in the see of Milan, had been exiled to Cappadocia, where he died in 374; with Basil's assistance his body was brought back to Milan.

Other Eastern Rules, such as Jerome's translation of the Rule of Pachomius, also reached the West. But none of these were regarded as providing the fixed type of monachism; very much was left to the discretion of the abbot, whose position was of much more importance than in later times[1]. Dom Butler describes the situation thus: "I do not know of any evidence that would lead us to suppose that the life of any monastery in Italy (or Western Europe) was organised on the lines of either system"—i.e. Basilian or Pachomian. "Italian monachism in the fifth century seems to have been eclectic in character, and to have freely borrowed ideas and regulations from these two Rules, and from other documents of Egyptian origin—from Cassian, the *Historia Monachorum*, the *Apophthegmata*, the *Regula Orientalis*, the *Regula Serapionis*, the *Regula Macarii*, the *Regula SS. Patrum*. St Benedict shows familiarity with all these documents; and this goes to prove that they were all in current use in the monasteries of Central Italy at the end of the fifth century[2]."

Cassian, who has been mentioned above, deserves a brief notice, since he was undoubtedly the most considerable figure in Western monasticism before Benedict[3]. After

---

[1] Cf. Spreitzenhofer, *op. cit.* p. 39, "In jedem Kloster der Wille des Abtes die oberste und öfter auch alleinige Regel darstellte."

[2] *Lausiac History*, I. 249.

[3] See Bp Gibson's prolegomena to his translation of Cassian in the *Nicene and post-Nicene Fathers*.

long-continued travels in the East he returned to Gaul and founded a monastery at Marseilles in the year 410, at the same time that Honoratus was organising his famous convent at Lerins. In his *Institutes* and *Conferences* Cassian gave the West a great storehouse of information on the customs of the Eastern monks. He was perhaps the first who really appreciated the difference between the physical constitutions of Eastern and Western men, and to a certain extent he followed Basil's lead in recommending to the latter a mitigation of austerities. At the end of the preface to the *Institutes* he says : " I shall however venture to exercise this discretion in my work—that where I find anything in the rule of the Egyptians which, either because of the severity of the climate, or owing to some difficulty or diversity of habits, is impossible in these countries, or hard or difficult, I shall to some extent balance it by the customs of the monasteries which are found throughout Pontus and Mesopotamia[1]." But he seems to have owed comparatively little to his study of the Basilian Rules. While there are many parallelisms in the thoughts of the two writers, cases of literary dependence of Cassian on the older writer are very few[2].

If Cassian saw that monasticism must be adapted to Western needs, the credit of taking the necessary steps in this direction must be ascribed to the famous Benedict of Nursia. Benedict was born about 480 and belonged to a noble family, like so many of his spiritual sons in later times. He was sent to Rome for his education, but some time about 500 he left the capital, disgusted with the vices of city life, and resolved to become a monk. He is said

---

[1] Pontus must refer to the Basilian monasteries. The austerities of Mesopotamian monachism, however, were if anything more severe than those practised in Egypt. See p. 42.

[2] The following seem to be clear cases : Cass., *Inst.* I. 1 = Basil, F. 23 (the girdle); *Inst.* I. 2 = F. 22 (the monk's dress); *Inst.* I. 6 = F. 22 (sheep-skin and goat-skin); *Inst.* IV. 17 = B. 180 (reading aloud at meals). In the last passage Cassian says expressly that it is a Cappadocian, not Egyptian, custom. B. 180 is not in Rufinus' version of Basil's Rules, so perhaps this is an exception to the statement that Basil's Rules were only known in the West through Rufinus. But the report may have reached Cassian orally.

to have spent three years of complete solitude in a cave, after which he came out and organised the disciples that had gathered round him into a monastery. Before long it became necessary to found a number of other monasteries in the neighbourhood. Benedict finally returned to Monte Cassino, where he presided over the foundation most closely connected with his name.

The revival of Western monachism that dated from Benedict was most opportune. A new impulse was sorely needed; while its general spirit was, as we have seen, thoroughly eclectic, yet it was generally understood that the lives of the Egyptian monks were suitable models for general imitation. But it had proved impossible for Western men to practise the austerities associated with their ideal, and so the general feeling was one of "discouragement and demoralisation consequent on an abiding sense of failure[1]." To meet the needs of the situation Benedict composed his famous Rule[2], which aimed at enforcing a moderate rule of life that would be practicable for all. Its leading features were the insistence on a common life, the elimination of individual austerities, the requiring of manual labour and study of Scripture, the careful regulation of the real *Work* of the community, namely the continual round of devotion, the forbidding of a monk to leave the monastery where he had been professed, and the definition of the abbot's position and powers—he was to be elected by the monks and had to consult with them, but the Rule was to guide him instead of, as heretofore, his own discretion. It is important to notice Benedict's attitude towards the eremitic life. He legislated only for cenobites, though he recognised the existence of the other ideal. His Rule is but "a little Rule for beginners" (*minima inchoationis regula*); but his own monks were precluded by their vow of *stabilitas* from passing over to a hermit life. He made no

---

[1] Butler, *Lausiac History*, I. 251.

[2] Dom Butler's edition (Freiburg, 1912), supersedes former editions. The English reader will find Dom Hunter-Blair's edition still useful (2nd ed. London, 1906). Miss Hodgson gives a most attractive account in *Ch. Quart. Rev.* Jan. 1912.

provision for any federation of monasteries. Each house was to be independent and self-sufficing.

The literary sources of the Benedictine Rule have been given by Dom Butler in his new edition. In a number of places Benedict has borrowed from Basil's Rules[1], but as regards details Cassian was by far the most important of his authorities. Cassian was nearer to him in point of time and had written for Western men; it was therefore only to be expected that Benedict should make more use of his writings. But he recommended for further study by his monks not only the books of the Bible, but the writings of the holy Catholic Fathers, the *Conferences* and *Institutes* (i.e. of Cassian) and "the Rule of our holy father Basil[2]." Basil is the only Father expressly named, and the fundamental principles of his monastic system were, in the main, reproduced by Benedict[3].

Let us look first at the similarities between the two Rules. Dr Dudden, in an admirable sketch of the Benedictine Rule, sees in it three main principles—absolute obedience, simplicity of living, and constant occupation[4]. This would serve equally well for a description of the Basilian Rule, though it would fail to express its special characteristics. If we go a little further in our inquiry, we find that both Rules inculcate unconditional obedience to the Superior, active work, and the practising of silence and humility; the regulations for the reception of new-comers into the community are

---

[1] The following parallels are extracted from Butler's notes. The Basilian Rules are referred to in Rufinus' version, through which they were known in the West (see Appendix B). Benedict, 2, lines 8—10=Bas. *Reg.* 15; Ben. 2, 68= Bas. 98; Ben. 7, 91—96=Bas. 12; Ben. 7, 157=Bas. 62; Ben. 20, 1 ff.=Bas. 108; Ben. 31, 19—20=Bas. 103, cf. 104 (tools, etc., are consecrated to God); Ben. 33, title=Bas. 29, title (should monks have private property?); Ben. 36, 1—5=Bas. 36; Ben. 40, 17=Bas. 9; Ben. 48, 1=Bas. 192 (*et Salomon : Otiositas inimica est animae,* not in Greek text, see p. 166); Ben. 50, 1—5=Bas. 107; Ben. 55, 13—14=Bas. 9; Ben. 55, 42—45=Bas. 94; Ben. 58, 14—16=Bas. 6; Ben. 58, 62=Bas. 106; Ben. 59, 22=Bas. 7; Ben. 61, 17=Bas. 192; Ben. 68, 4—8=Bas. 69.

[2] C. 73.

[3] So Butler, *Enc. Brit.* art. "Basilian Monks": "St Benedict owed more of the ground-ideas of his Rule to St Basil than to any other monastic legislator."

[4] *Gregory the Great*, I. 109—114.

essentially the same in both. Both allow boys within the monastery, and forbid the holding of property by individuals. In each Rule great disciplinary powers are given to the abbot, and exclusion from the community is ordained as the punishment of a contumacious monk[1].

The main differences between the two Rules are these. Basil is primarily a preacher, Benedict a legislator. Basil lays down general principles and leaves their application to the Superior, Benedict gives precise directions. Thus Benedict has definite regulations for the clothes of the monks, the hours of meals, the quality and amount of food, the number of fasts, and the titles of the various officers, all of which are left undefined in Basil[2]. In some respects Benedict is actually opposed to Basil. Basil's convents are directly responsible for philanthropic work and so must be in the neighbourhood of towns; visits to relations and friends are allowed under due safeguards; short term vows are contemplated in certain cases; a monk once excluded is never to be readmitted; wine is forbidden under normal circumstances. Benedict on the contrary requires complete separation from the world, and a permanent vow of *stabilitas*; a lapsed monk may be readmitted as many as three times before his final exclusion; wine is allowed as part of a much milder regime than had hitherto been approved by any monastic legislator.

It is clear that the resemblances between the two Rules are more important than the differences. Benedict owed much to Basil. He adopted his main ideas, modifying them however in the direction of "greater isolation from the world and a milder regime of convent life[3]." There is little that is original in Benedict's Rule, unless a talent for selection and adaptation to local needs is a sign of originality. But the

---

[1] This paragraph and the next are taken from Grützmacher, *Die Bedeutung Benedikts von Nursia und seiner Regel in der Geschichte des Mönchtums*, pp. 40 ff. On some points the statements (in respect of Basil's Rules) need qualification, see p. 93 of this book for checks on the Superior's power, and p. 82 for the holding of property.

[2] Grützmacher's remark on p. 42 is an over-statement, "Das Verhältnis des Kloster zum Diöcesanbischof findet sich an keiner Stelle bei Basilius berührt." See p. 102.

[3] Grützmacher, *op. cit.* p. 44.

Benedictine Rule, if less original than the Basilian, is superior to it in every direction as a practical guide for the monastic life. By its intrinsic merits it won a unique position in the West, and remained for many centuries the dominating influence in monasticism.

In Ireland, however, a different form of monachism prevailed, marked by enthusiastic missionary fervour and rigorous austerities. One peculiar feature of Irish asceticism was the existence of double monasteries. It is conceivable that Rufinus' version of Basil's Rules, with its description of the similar system in Cappadocia, had reached the far West. But it is much more likely that the phenomenon appeared independently in two places, under analogous conditions of primitive enthusiasm[1].

In conclusion, one final question may be asked. What was the fate in the West of those ideals which were Basil's own special contribution to monasticism? These were, so we have seen above[2], the establishment of cenobitism as the highest and, apparently, the sole legitimate form of monachism, the bringing into its service of the best culture of the time, and the employment of the monks in works of practical usefulness, such as the education of the young and the relief of physical suffering.

In regard to the first of these, Benedict's definition of the solitaries, or second class of monks, makes it plain that he shared the prevailing view, that the cenobium was a kind of school in which the monk could learn the rudiments of asceticism, after which he could proceed to the higher stage of solitude[3]. However, he did not allow his own monks to pass over to the solitary life, and thus he agreed with Basil in practice, if not in theory. In the second place, Benedict, like Basil, was of noble family and good education, and many of

---

[1] Cf. p. 105.                     [2] pp. 123—126.

[3] "Deinde secundum genus est anachoritarum, id est heremitarum, horum qui non conversationis fervore novicio sed monasterii probatione diuturna, qui didicerunt contra diabolum multorum solacio iam docti pugnare; et bene extructi fraterna ex acie ad singularem pugnam heremi securi iam sine consolatione alterius, sola manu vel brachio contra vitia carnis vel cogitationum Deo auxiliante pugnare sufficiunt." *Reg. Ben.* 1.

his followers resembled him in this particular. In his Rule the daily study of Scripture and the Fathers was enjoined, and the great services rendered to humanity in later centuries by the literary labours of the Benedictines have their root ultimately in this regulation of their founder. But the third of Basil's ideals was not realised in the legislation of Benedict. Whilst there are many references to boys in the Benedictine Rule, which presuppose their presence in the monastery, there is no express mention of a school such as we find in Basil. And again, Benedict gives regulations for the reception of guests, but these are apparently visitors who have come for edification; the remoteness of the monasteries from the outside world prevented the monks from undertaking such works of mercy as Basil had prescribed to his followers.

If Basil's ideals were only partially realised in Benedict, they have been triumphantly vindicated by the course of later Church history; the most fruitful developments of Western monasticism have been on the lines laid down by him. Cenobitism under various forms has become the one recognised type of Western asceticism, and the solitary life has practically ceased to exist. New Orders, such as the Jesuits and Christian Brothers, have arisen, which have put the education of the young in the forefront of their policy; while the teaching sisterhoods have played an important part in the education of girls in most Western countries. And, finally, the work done by women ascetics in hospitals and orphanages and in the poorest parts of big towns has won the admiration of the outside world. "Sisters of Mercy" are honoured and loved in quarters where there is little or no appreciation of the ideals of the ascetic life.

We do not pretend that Basil had anything to do with these later developments, but there is a striking resemblance between his ideals and those of modern times. In some respects he was in advance of his age; certainly he was the most modern among the pioneers of monasticism, and for this reason, if for none other, his work has a permanent interest for the student of asceticism.

# CHAPTER X

OUR study of St Basil and his influence on the later Church is now complete. However, in view of certain widespread misconceptions on the subject, it seems well to add a few words on the real meaning of asceticism, and the value of its ideals for the modern world.

In the foregoing pages we have dwelt almost entirely on the external side of Basil's monastic work, and laid considerable stress on the practical activities which he required from his monks. This was natural, seeing that the special interest of the subject lies in this direction. But it must not be thought that Basil was inspired by motives different from those which have actuated other leaders of asceticism. All alike have had one primary object, the love of God. The love of man has followed from this in most cases as a necessary deduction. In some writers—Basil for example—it has been insisted on with more emphasis than in others; but it has always remained a secondary object. What Dom Butler says of Benedict and his monks is equally true of Basil: "His idea simply was to make them *good*: and if a man *is* good, he will *do* good[1]." The fundamental idea of monasticism has always been that the attainment of the knowledge and love of God is a matter of such importance as to demand the dedication of the whole life. The progress of the great world outside, the triumphs of secular civilisation, even the noble task which lies before the Church as a whole, of consecrating to the service of God the treasures of art,

[1] *Camb. Med. Hist.* I. 540.

science and literature—all these are not primarily for the monk objects of interest. His concern is with the unseen and eternal world. If activities beneficial to the Church and world grow out of his life, so much the better. But he does not set out with the conscious intention of improving the world.

It is clear that such an ideal is strongly opposed to the prevailing spirit of the age. "Other-worldly" is frequently used as a term of reproach, and even devout Christians often condemn the monk's life for its "uselessness[1]." And yet the modern world speaks with two voices in this matter. There are some to whom the idea of a monastery appeals with irresistible force; there rises in their mind the vision of a haunt of ancient peace, and a desire to flee away and be at rest. Who can deny the beauty of Cardinal Newman's words[2]?

"To the monk heaven was next door; he formed no plans, he had no cares; the ravens of his father Benedict were ever at his side. He 'went forth' in his youth 'to his work and to his labour' until the evening of life; if he lived a day longer, he did a day's work more; whether he lived many days or few, he laboured on to the end of them. He had no wish to see further in advance of his journey than where he was to make his next stage. He ploughed and sowed, he prayed, he meditated, he studied, he wrote, he taught, and then he died and went to heaven."

But let us put aside sentimental considerations and ask what value the ideals of ascetism have for our own age and country. Our remarks will have reference only to the Church of England. The problem hardly arises in the English and Scotch Protestant bodies; whilst it would be obviously impertinent for one who is not a member of the Roman Catholic Church to discuss modern Roman monasticism, unless he

[1] The reproach sometimes levelled against monasticism, that its teaching on marriage is anti-social, comes with an ill grace from a society in which perhaps a hundred remain permanently unmarried from economic motives for every one that is a celibate on religious grounds.

[2] *Historical Sketches*, II. 426, quoted by Miss Hodgson in *Ch. Quart. Rev.* Jan. 1912.

had a very intimate acquaintance with the subject. If monasticism is indigenous, so to speak, in the Roman Church, in the Anglican it is perhaps still an exotic. The average Churchman considers it a sort of resuscitated medievalism, and quietly disapproves, or perhaps tolerates it as a convenient method of getting cheap clergy, teachers or nurses. It is seldom that he reflects on the underlying principles of the monastic life.

A clear distinction must be drawn between asceticism and monasticism. Asceticism is a necessary element in all the higher religions, and implies severe self-discipline exercised for religious ends in regard to the natural desires of the body and the attractions of the outside world. Monasticism is the special form which, owing to a variety of causes, the ascetic spirit assumed in the fourth century A.D.[1] Now the particular phase of thought in which Christianity and asceticism were practically interchangeable terms has long passed away. But the ascetic ideal has not ceased to be an element in Christianity, and at the present day its importance is considerable. If the Church is to remain loyal to its Founder, it must not neglect the other-worldly element in His teaching. It can best ensure that a proper emphasis is laid on this, if it has in its midst numbers of men and women pledged to a preoccupation with the unseen world. There is no fear that we shall have too many ascetics. But this is an age of specialisation, and the monk has as legitimate a place as the philosopher or professor. His very existence bears witness to an unseen world.

But it does not necessarily follow that the traditional monastic system is the method of practising asceticism best suited to modern Europeans. In the realm of dogmatics, the decrees of Chalcedon are of great value to the student, and are regarded by some minds as permanently valid conclusions. But there remain many who feel the need of modern categories of thought to express their convictions about God and Christ. Similarly in the case of asceticism. In the Roman Catholic Church the stream will continue to flow in the channel cut

[1] See Chapter I.

deep by the tradition of centuries. But is it necessary for the Anglican Church to revive customs and methods which are frequently unsuited to the constitutions and mental habits of twentieth century Englishmen?

While appreciating to the full the benefits bestowed on the Church by existing communities, one would rather see arising in the future societies of men and women, not bound by the Western monastic tradition, but allowing themselves the fullest freedom both in adapting old rules, and experimenting in new directions. There is much in the Basilian literature that might provide hints for such a development. The spirit of the English race is akin in many ways to that of Greece rather than Rome, and a study of St Basil, the father of Greek monasticism, may be not unprofitable for the English Church of to-day.

# APPENDIX A

## EUSTATHIUS OF SEBASTE

IN the body of the book mention has been made of Eustathius on several occasions (pp. 24, 46, 47), but it seemed advisable to defer any connected account of him to an appendix.

He was much older than Basil, having been born about the beginning of the fourth century. In his youth he studied at Alexandria under Arius. After some rebuffs on account of his heretical antecedents, he succeeded at length in getting ordained. By 357 he had become bishop of Sebaste. His death occurred in 379, shortly after Basil's.

His career has a double interest, doctrinal and ascetic; in both respects it was closely interwoven with the life of Basil, and in fact apart from Basil's letters our knowledge of him is scanty. The traditional presentation of Eustathius has charged him with a fundamental lack of principle, and depicted him as a kind of doctrinal chameleon, ready to change his colours on the slightest provocation and sign any and every doctrinal formula.

Such an interpretation, popular as it has been, is difficult to reconcile with certain other facts. Epiphanius records the admiration which many felt for his manner of life (τὸν βίον αὐτοῦ καὶ τὴν πολιτείαν οὐκ ὀλίγοι ἄνδρες θαυμάζουσιν, *Haer.* 75, 2), while Philostorgius, the Arian historian, puts Eustathius in the front rank of the anti-Arian champions (τῶν τὸ ὁμοούσιον δοξαζόντων...Εὐστάθιος, γηραιὸς ἀνὴρ καὶ τῷ πλήθει αἰδοῖός τε καὶ πιθανός, Migne, *P. G.* LXV. 568). Is the traditional verdict on Eustathius, drawn from Basil's statements, consistent with the high reputation which he undoubtedly enjoyed, and the genuine religious influence which he exercised over large numbers of disciples?

The problem has been treated by Loofs in his fine monograph, *Eustathius von Sebaste und die Chronologie der Basilius-Briefe* (Halle, 1898), in which he points out that historians have judged Eustathius by what Basil wrote in the heat of a bitter controversy, and have failed to make allowances for Basil's partisanship. So he makes a fresh investigation into the causes of the quarrel between the two men, with the following results.

The breach took place in 372. Before this date Basil had been friendly and even enthusiastic towards Eustathius. If his subsequent reproaches were justified, his conduct towards Eustathius before 372 deserved condemnation, for he must have condoned wrong-doing. The exact occasion of the quarrel is obscure, but the cause clear enough. Eustathius remained faithful to the *middle* party of Homoiousians (τῆς μεσότητος οὐδὲν αὐτῷ γέγονε προτιμότερον, Bas. *Ep.* 128). He had moved a long way from his original Arian position, and come finally to interpret Homoiousios in the sense of Homoousios, so far as the Son was concerned. But when Basil and the "young-Nicene" party went on to predicate Homoousios of the Spirit, he could not follow them. The immediate occasion of the quarrel may have been either friction over metropolitan rights, or the question of Meletius, or perhaps both combined. Sebaste, as metropolis of Roman Armenia, had rights over Nicopolis, and Basil had been interfering in the affairs of Nicopolis ; while again the feud between Eustathius and Meletius was of long standing and might easily cause trouble. Meletius had once taken Eustathius' place as bishop of Sebaste, but could not retain his position. The exigencies of ecclesiastical controversy and Basil's relations with the West forced him to propitiate Antiochian public opinion. Having to choose between Eustathius and Meletius, he preferred the latter, and thus sacrificed an old friendship to the necessities of Church politics.

Such is Loofs' interpretation of the events. Duchesne makes the obvious remark: "À certains endroits l'auteur dépasse un peu la mesure, entraîné par son ardeur de réhabilitation" (*Histoire ancienne*, II. 381), and Schäfer (*Basilius des Grossen Beziehungen zum Abendlande*) criticises his results in a few details ; but the main conclusions of the book do not seem to have been refuted. All the same, Eustathius must have been a most annoying person to anyone who was endowed with a clear intellectual vision and could see what was really involved in the settlement of the doctrinal controversies. Perhaps the best defence of him is that he was eminently a practical man. "His life belonged to the ascetic ideal," and his interest in doctrine was only secondary.

The ascetic side of his life is of more importance for our purposes, and now requires consideration. We have already described the part played by Eustathius in the development of Basil's monastic ideals (pp. 46, 47). It is clear that Basil owed much to his teacher, but precisely how much it is difficult to say. Two points remain for a brief discussion here, (*a*) the bearing of Sozomen's evidence on the authenticity of Basil's *Ascetica*, and (*b*) the Synod of Gangra.

(*a*) Sozomen, *H. E.* III. 14, reports that some considered Eustathius to be the author of the ascetic book (ἀσκητικὴ βίβλος) commonly attributed to Basil. This is an important piece of evidence and may be accepted as quite trustworthy. An orthodox fifth century historian would not have reported a mere idle rumour assigning the works of a great Doctor of the

Church to his heretical opponent. What then did the tradition assert? It refers to the *corpus asceticum* of Basil, and not to one particular book. The ascetic book (τὸ ἀσκητικόν) of Basil as known to Jerome and Rufinus consisted of the Longer and Shorter Rules. When Photius wrote, the *Ascetica* of Basil were in two volumes, or rather, one volume with a short introduction; it contained the Rules, Morals and some tracts (see pp. 65, 66). The extent of Sozomen's ἀσκητικὴ βίβλος must remain uncertain. Garnier's attempt to make it refer to the *Constitutiones Monasticae* was quite unsuccessful (p. 79). Sozomen asserts therefore that an undefined body of ascetic writings inscribed with Basil's name was attributed by some to Eustathius. Such an opinion was of course erroneous; but it contained an important element of truth. Basil owed much to Eustathius, and the teaching and practices of the latter must have been to some extent represented in Basil's *Ascetica*; so much so that those who recalled Eustathius' teaching and championed his memory could say that the ideas were really his. It was but a short step to take when they or others went on to ascribe the actual writing to him. Just how much is Eustathian it is impossible to say, but it is safe to assert with Loofs: "in Basilius' corpus asceticum ein gut Teil geistigen Eigentums des Eustathius steckt" (*op. cit.* p. 97).

(*b*) The date of the Council of Gangra has been a vexed question, but c. 340 seems to be generally accepted at the present time. The bishops dealt with certain excesses of asceticism, practised by the followers of Eustathius. If it could be shown that the Eustathian tenets, as described in the synodical letter and accompanying Canons, are radically different from the positions taken up by Basil, the result reached above with reference to the Eustathian element in Basil's *Ascetica* would be seriously shaken. But the following considerations make such a conclusion improbable.

(i) There is no need to ascribe all the eccentricities condemned at Gangra to Eustathius personally, for

(*a*) Soz. *H. E.* III. 14, expressly says that some considered Eustathius to be free from blame.

(*b*) The synodical letter of the Council makes it plain that the *followers* of Eustathius, not the master himself, were responsible for the excesses (εὕρισκεν πολλὰ ἀθέσμως γινόμενα ὑπὸ τούτων αὐτῶν τῶν περὶ Εὐστάθιον, Mansi, II. 1097).

(ii) Basil supported Eustathius when accusations of heresy were brought against him (see *Epp.* 223, 3; 244, 1). Notice also Basil's silence on the subject of this condemnation at Gangra.

(iii) Complaints of encouraging disorder by his monastic innovations were made against Basil (see Bas. *Ep.* 207; cf. Greg. Nyss. *in Eun.* I. 10).

L. C. 11

(iv)　Basil's own teaching with reference to the reception of married persons and slaves in the convent is very similar to the positions condemned by the Council of Gangra (see pp. 84, 85).

The conclusion therefore is fully justified, that the ascetic teaching of Eustathius and Basil may be for practical purposes regarded as identical.

## APPENDIX B

### RUFINUS' EDITION OF BASIL'S RULES

Tyrannius Rufinus was born about 345 in the neighbourhood of Aquileia.　He received his early ascetic education in a monastery of that town.　In 371 he went to the East and remained there till 397, when he returned to Italy.　On his return Urseius, abbot of Pinetum near Ravenna, asked for information about the monasteries of the East.　Rufinus told him of Basil's answers to the questions of his monks.　(*Ad quae ego ne quid tibi minus digne, non dico quam geritur, sed quam geri debet, exponerem, S. Basilii Cappadociae episcopi, viri fide et operibus et omni sanctitate satis clari, instituta monachorum, quae interrogantibus se monachis velut sancti cuiusdem iuris responsa statuit, protuli.*)　Urseius was much interested in what he heard, and Rufinus accordingly translated the work into Latin, assuring Urseius that the practice of the Rules in the monasteries of the West (*per universa occiduae partis monasteria*) would be beneficial.　He bids Urseius have copies made and sent to other monasteries, in order that all the monasteries may live according to the same rules, and follow the lead of Cappadocia.　(*Tui sane sit officium etiam aliis monasteriis exemplaria praebere: ut secundum instar Cappadociae omnia monasteria eisdem et non diversis vel institutis vel observationibus vivant.*)

This translation is not given in the editions of Rufinus, and must be looked for in Lucas Holstenius' *Codex Regularum* (Paris, 1663), or in Brockie's later edition of 1759.　It is also printed in Migne, *P.L.* CIII. 485—554.　Rufinus refers elsewhere (*H.E.* II. 9) to his translation of Basil's Rules, and expresses a hope that he may be able to translate more of his works.　(*Extant quoque utriusque*—i.e., Basil and Gregory— *monumenta magnifica tractatuum, quos ex tempore in ecclesiis declamabant: ex quibus nos denas ferme singulorum oratiunculas transfudimus in Latinam; Basilii praeterea instituta monachorum: optantes, si poterimus et dei favor adiuverit, eorum plura transferre.*)　This translation is a conflation of the 55 Longer and 313 Shorter Rules to make one book of 203 Rules[1].

---

[1] Zöckler, *Askese und Mönchtum*, p. 286, says wrongly that Rufinus 1—15 correspond to Basil's Longer Rules, 16—203 to the Shorter.

The following tables will show how Rufinus treated his materials:

I. *The Rules of Rufinus with the corresponding Rules of Basil* (F.=*fusius tractatae*, B.=*brevius tractatae*).

| Rufinus | Basil | | Rufinus | Basil |
|---|---|---|---|---|
| Preface = | {Preface to B. (all) | | 24 = | B. 158 |
| | {Preface to F. (conclusion)[1] | | 25 | 159 |
| I | F. 1 | | 26 | 7 |
| | ⎧ 2 | | 27 | 8 |
| | ⎪ 3 | | 28 | 9 |
| 2 | ⎨ 4 | | 29 | 85 |
| | ⎪ 5 | | 30 | 86 |
| | ⎩ 6[2] | | 31 | 187 |
| 3 | 7[3] | | 32 | 188 |
| 4 | 8[2] | | 33 | 189 |
| 5 | 9[2] | | 34 | 21 |
| 6 | 10[3] | | 35 | 22 |
| 7 | {14 | | 36 | 160 |
| | {15[4] | | 37 | 161 |
| 8 | {16 | | 38 | 162 |
| | {17 | | 39 | 163 |
| 9 | 19 | | 40 | 23 |
| 10 | {21 | | 41 | 24 |
| | {24[5] | | 42 | 25 |
| 11 | {22 | | 43 | 26 |
| | {23 | | 44 | 27 |
| 12 | B. 1 | | 45 | 28 |
| 13 | 114[6] | | 46 | 29 |
| 14 | 157 | | 47 | 191 |
| 15 | 184[7] | | 48 | 126 |
| 16 | 3 | | 49 | 30 |
| 17 | 4 | | 50 | 192 |
| 18 | 5 | | 51 | 193 |
| 19 | 287[8] | | 52 | 194 |
| 20 | 6 | | 53 | 31 |
| 21 | 288 | | 54 | 88 |
| 22 | 289 | | 55 | 32 |
| 23 | 99 | | 56 | 195 |

[1] The portion of F. used is nearly equal in length to the whole of B. The two parts are neatly joined.      [2] Much shortened.      [3] Shortened.

[4] Rufinus uses the question and part of the answer of F. 15, with the concluding words of F. 14.

[5] Rufinus concludes with the opening words (a biblical quotation) of F. 24.

[6] The quotation at the end of Ruf. 12 begins the question in B. 114.

[7] Rufinus adapts and improves with great freedom.

[8] The question in B. 287 repeats the second half of the question in B. 5.

| Rufinus | Basil | | Rufinus | Basil |
|---|---|---|---|---|
| 57 = | B. 196 | | 101 = | B. 141 |
| 58 | 197 | | 102 | 142 |
| 59 | 33 | | 103 | 143 |
| 60 | 34 | | 104 | 144 |
| 61 | 35 | | 105 | 145 |
| 62 | 198 | | 106 | 146 |
| 63 | 36 | | 107 | 147 |
| 64 | 115 | | 108 | 201 |
| 65 | 116 | | 109 | 202 |
| 66 | 37 | | 110 | 279 |
| 67 | 117 | | 111 | 148 |
| 68 | 118 | | 112 | 149 |
| 69 | 119 | | 113 | 150 |
| 70 | 38 | | 114 | 203 |
| 71 | 39 | | 115 | 170 |
| 72 | 40 | | 116 | 171 |
| 73 | 41 | | 117 | 10 |
| 74 | 42 | | 118 | 89 |
| 75 | 43 | | 119 | 45 |
| 76 | 44 | | 120 | 283 |
| 77 | 164 | | 121 | 46 |
| 78 | 165 | | 122 | 47 |
| 79 | 127 | | 123 | 16 |
| 80 | 120 | | 124 | 204 |
| 81 | 96 | | 125 | 205 |
| 82 | 121 | | 126 | 206 |
| 83 | 199 | | 127 | 207 |
| 84 | 166 | | 128 | 17 |
| 85 | 167 | | 129 | 90 |
| 86 | 200 | | 130 | 151 |
| 87 | 97 | | 131 | 152 |
| 88 | 128 | | 132 | 153 |
| 89 | 129 | | 133 | 122 |
| 90 | 130 | | 134 | 172 |
| 91 | 131 | | 135 | 239 |
| 92 | 132 | | 136 | 208 |
| 93 | 133 | | 137 | 173 |
| 94 | 135 | | 138 | 209 |
| 95 | 168 | | 139 | 240 |
| 96 | 134 | | 140 | 241 |
| 97 | 136 | | 141 | 48 |
| 98 | 100 | | 142 | 49 |
| 99 | 87 | | 143 | 210 |
| 100 | 169 | | 144 | 50 |

| Rufinus | Basil | Rufinus | Basil |
|---|---|---|---|
| 145 = B. | 51 | 175 = B. | 57 |
| 146 | 52 | 176 | 123 |
| 147 | 53 | 177 | 177 |
| 148 | 280 | 178 | 178 |
| 149 | 11 | 179 | 221 |
| 150 | 174 | 180 | 222 |
| 151 | 211 | 181 | 137 |
| 152 | 212 | 182 | 58 |
| 153 | 213 | 183 | 59 |
| 154 | 54 | 184 | 60 |
| 155 | 175 | 185 | 101 |
| 156 | 176 | 186 | 91 |
| 157 | 243 | 187 | 179 |
| 158 | 244 | 188 | 62 |
| 159 | 55 | 189 | 67 |
| 160 | 215 | 190 | 68 |
| 161 | 216 | 191 | 182 |
| 162 | 245 | 192 | 105[1] |
| 163 | 217 | 193 | 73 |
| 164 | 56 | 194 | 106 |
| 165 | 246 | 195 | 75 |
| 166 | 247 | 196 | 94 |
| 167 | 218 | 197 | 108 |
| 168 | 248 | 198 | 109 |
| 169 | 219 | 199 | 110 |
| 170 | 249 | 200 | 229 |
| 171 | 250 | 201 | 111[1] |
| 172 | 251 | 202 | 275 |
| 173 | 252 | 203 | 274 |
| 174 | 220 | | |

II.  *Rules of Basil omitted altogether by Rufinus.*
*Longer Rules* (F.) 11—13, 18, 20, 25—55.

*Shorter Rules* (B.) 2, 12—15, 18—20, 61, 63—66, 69—72, 74, 76—84 92, 93, 95, 98, 102—104, 107, 112, 113, 124, 125, 138—140, 154—156, 180, 181, 183, 185, 186, 190, 214, 223—228, 230—238, 242, 253—273, 276—278, 281, 282, 284—286, 290—313.

III.  *Totals.*

| Basil's Rules | Longer | Shorter |
|---|---|---|
| Represented in Rufinus | 19 | 192 |
| Omitted by Rufinus | 36 | 121 |
| | 55 | 313 |

[1] Rufinus expands considerably.

In the course of studying Rufinus' translation with the view of throwing some light on the textual history of the Basilian Rules, I made the foregoing tables for my own use. I have inserted them at this point, because, so far as I am aware, the information contained in them does not exist elsewhere in print. The following conclusions seem to be justified by a study of the evidence.

Rufinus apparently had the two sets of Rules before him in one book, which he calls *hoc opus* in the Preface. His general principle was to abbreviate; the Shorter Rules suited his purpose best, and he was able to use these almost as they stood, sometimes even expanding them. But the Longer Rules were subjected to a drastic revision and condensation; Rufinus' second Rule, for example, represents F. 2—6. Throughout his version, but especially in his treatment of F., Rufinus paraphrases and adapts with considerable freedom, and even introduces a certain amount of matter of his own. The changes, however, are of little importance; one of the chief is the occasional introduction of a different text from Scripture to support Basil's thesis.

Since the order of Ruf. 1—11 is practically identical with that of F. 1—24, it seems clear that F. lay before Rufinus in the same order as that of our modern editions. This agrees with the conclusion reached in Chapter V[1], with regard to the textual history, namely, that F. was put into literary form either by Basil himself, or more probably by a literary executor soon after Basil's death. But why did Rufinus stop short at the beginning of F. 24, and not revert to the Longer Rules again? It is conceivable that his MS stopped short at this point, but there are no other considerations to favour such a hypothesis. There is nothing in the style of the second half of F. to support the conclusion that it was added by a later hand. Nor need any importance be attached to the fact that a break occurs in the text at the point where Rufinus leaves off. The personal element has been absent for some time from the questions, but the question in F. 24 runs as follows: "Now that these things have been sufficiently explained to us, our next task should be to learn the character of our life with one another" (τούτων ἱκανῶς ἡμῖν παραδεδομένων, ἀκόλουθον ἂν εἴη μαθεῖν ἡμᾶς περὶ τοῦ τρόπου τῆς μετ' ἀλλήλων διαγωγῆς). But as similar expressions occur in F. 38 and 43, it would not be right to lay stress on the one in F. 24. Besides, Rufinus evidently had F. 24 before him, since in his 11th Rule, founded on F. 21, he has a biblical quotation (1 Cor. xiv. 40) drawn from F. 24. We conclude that the presence of a mark of transition just where Rufinus breaks off is a mere coincidence.

Rufinus followed the Longer Rules for a while, and then, owing to reasons unknown to us, passed on to the Shorter. It is possible however to hazard a plausible guess as to his motives. He has already omitted F. 11 and 12, concerned with the reception into the convent of slaves and married people, perhaps because they were not applicable to the local circumstances of North Italy. After F. 24, where he finally deserts the Longer Rules, follow seven consecutive answers all dealing with the position and duties of the Superior (25—31). A number of subsequent answers are concerned, directly or indirectly, with the same topic (43—51, 54). Up to this point there have been only indirect references to the Superior. As Rufinus was writing for the abbot of Pinetum, he may have thought it unwise to translate a number of regulations about the abbot, some of which might have been sufficiently opposed to Urseius' practice as to cause him embarrassment.

The textual problems connected with Rufinus' use of the Shorter Rules are insoluble without an amount of study that I have been unable to give. I can only record my impressions. These Rules in their present form are quite devoid of any plan or arrangement. This need not affect our judgment of their authenticity, for their condition agrees with the presumed circumstances of their origin[1]. Rufinus omits many of the later Rules, very few of the earlier. B. 287—313 are absent from one manuscript[2], and their originality might therefore be suspected; but as they are represented in Rufinus it follows that he had the whole of B. before him. Where he omits material, it is either of little importance, or else of great interest for our knowledge of Cappadocian cenobitism, but for that very reason inapplicable to Western conditions. I see no grounds for thinking that the order of the Shorter Rules in Rufinus' MS was materially different from that of Garnier's edition. The evidence of the tables seems rather to point to the conclusion that he had the same order, and made a somewhat half-hearted and hasty attempt to arrange the material better. For example, Rufinus' Rules 16—28 are all concerned with penitence and the correction of offences, a subject of perennial interest to the Western Church, while there is a distinct effort to group the explanations of Scriptural passages. But Rufinus does not succeed in modifying to any great extent the motley nature of the work.

To conclude; Rufinus' translation is our oldest authority for the text of Basil's Rules. His evidence is not so full as we should like, since he only aims at giving extracts. But, so far as it goes, it proves that the Rules existed in their present form and were ascribed to Basil a few years after his death[3].

---

[1] See p. 73.        [2] See Garnier, *in loc.*

[3] Zöckler, *op. cit.* p. 290, states that the admissibility of double monasteries can be derived from Basil's regulations, and that the step was actually taken by Rufinus in his translation. But Basil describes an organised system which already existed (cf. p. 104). There is no advance whatever in Rufinus, who follows him closely on this point.

It is interesting to notice Rufinus' rendering of the question in B. 199 (εἰ χρὴ ἐξομολογουμένης ἀδελφῆς τῷ πρεσβυτέρῳ καὶ τὴν πρεσβυτέραν παρεῖναι). Garnier translates rightly, "An sorore seniori confitente, adesse oporteat etiam ipsam seniorem." From Rufinus' version ("Si oportet, cum aliqua soror confitetur quodcunque delictum suum presbytero, etiam matrem monasterii adesse?") no conception could be gained of the peculiar position of the senior members of the Basilian convent (see pp. 94 ff.).

## APPENDIX C

### A TABLE OF DATES

[The dates which mark the history of Egyptian Monasticism are taken, by kind permission of Dom E. C. Butler, from the second volume of his *Lausiac History*; the others from many different sources. Mr Johnston's edition of Basil's *De Spiritu Sancto* (Oxford, 1892) contains a very full table of dates for the doctrinal history of the fourth century.]

| | |
|---|---|
| c. 250 | Egyptian Christians flee to desert during Decian persecution. |
| 270 | Antony adopts ascetic life |
| 305 | Antony comes out from his cave and instructs disciples in monasticism. |
| c. 310 | Hilarion after a visit to Antony inaugurates Palestinian monasticism. |
| 314 | Pachomius becomes a monk. |
| c. 318 | Pachomius founds first Christian monastery at Tabennisi. |
| c. 325 | Mar Awgin founds monastery at Nisibis; beginning of Syriac monachism. |
| 320—330. | Amoun inaugurates Nitrian monachism. |
| c. 329 | Basil born. |
| 340 | Athanasius propagates monastic idea in Italy. |
| 346 | Death of Pachomius. |
| 351 | Basil goes to Athens. |
| 355, 356 | Basil returns to Caesarea. |
| 357, 358 | Basil visits Egypt. |
| 358 | Basil's first retirement to Pontus. |
| 360 | Basil at Council of Constantinople. |
| c. 361 | Basil writes *Moralia*. |
| 362 | Death of Dianius, bishop of Caesarea. Succession of Eusebius. Basil ordained priest (?). |
| 363—365 | Basil's second retirement in Pontus. Organises monasticism. Gives Longer Rules. |
| 365 | Basil returns to Caesarea. |
| 365—370 | Basil founds famous hospital at Caesarea. |
| 370 | Basil bishop of Caesarea. |
| c. 375 | Basil gives Shorter Rules. |
| 379 | Death of Basil. |
| 381 | Council of Constantinople. Triumph of Nicene orthodoxy. |
| 397 | Rufinus returns to Italy and translates Basil's Rules. |
| 463 | Foundation of the Studium. |
| c. 500 | Benedict becomes a monk. |
| 527 | Accession of Justinian. |
| c. 650 | Extensive Greek immigration into Sicily and Italy. |
| 789 | Theodore becomes abbot of Studium. |

| c. 850 | Beginnings of Basilian monachism in Calabria. |
|---|---|
| 850—900 | Beginnings of monachism on Mount Athos. |
| 1002 | Foundation of Grotta Ferrata. |
| c. 1374 | Beginnings of idiorrhythmic movement on Mount Athos. |
| 1446 | Bessarion General of Basilian Order. |
| 1573 | Gregory XIII reforms Basilian Order. |

# APPENDIX D

## BIBLIOGRAPHY

[The most important of the books consulted in the preparation of the foregoing chapters are given in the following lists. One or two are of a popular character, but have proved useful in pointing the way to larger or more detailed works.]

### The General History of Monasticism.

Besse, J. M. *Les Moines d'Orient.* Paris, 1900.

Butler, E. C. Article "Monasticism" in *Camb. Medieval History* (vol. I. c. 18). Cambridge, 1911.

Duchesne, L. *Histoire ancienne de l'Église* (vol. II. c. 14, *Les Moines d'Orient*). Paris, 1907.

Hannay, J. O. *The Spirit and Origin of Christian Monasticism.* London, 1903.

Harnack, A. *Monasticism*, Eng. Tr. London, 1901.

Heimbucher, M. *Die Orden und Kongregationen der katholischen Kirche* (2nd ed.). Paderborn, 1907.

Leclercq, H. Article "Cénobitisme" in *Dictionnaire d'Archéologie chrétienne.* Paris, 1910.

Smith, I. G. *Christian Monasticism from the Fourth to the Ninth Centuries.* London, 1892.

Zöckler, O. *Askese und Mönchtum.* Frankfurt a.M., 1897.

### Egyptian Monasticism.

Amélineau, E. *Étude historique sur saint Pachome.* 1887.

Bornemann. *In investiganda Monachatus origine quibus de causis ratio habenda sit Origenis.* Göttingen, 1885.

Butler, E. C. *The Lausiac History of Palladius.* Cambridge, 1904.

Ladeuze, P. *Étude sur le Cénobitisme pakhomien.* Louvain, 1898.

Lucot, A. *Palladius, Histoire Lausiaque.* Paris, 1912.

Preuschen, E. *Mönchtum und Sarapiskult.* Giessen, 1903.

Robertson (Bp), A. Athanasius' *Life of Antony* in Nicene Fathers' Library. Oxford, 1892.

Watson, E. W. "Palladius and Egyptian Monasticism" (*Church Quarterly Review*). April, 1907.

## St Basil.

Allard, P.   *Saint Basile* (5th ed.).   Paris, 1903.

Boulenger, F.   *Grégoire Nazianze, Discours funèbres.*   Paris, 1908.

Ceillier.   *Histoire Générale* (VI. 161—195).   Paris, 1729—1763.

Fialon, E.   *Étude sur Saint Basile* (2nd ed.).   Paris, 1869.

Garnier.   *Opera Basilii.*   Paris, 1721—1730.   The 3rd vol. is edited by Maran.   Reprinted 1839; also in Migne, *P.G.* XXIX.—XXXII.   Paris, 1857.

Holl, R.   *Enthusiasmus und Bussgewalt beim griechischen Mönchtum* (pp. 156—170).   Leipzig, 1898.

Holsten, L.   *Codex Regularum.*   Paris, 1663.

Jackson, B.   Translation of Basil's letters and some other works in Nicene Fathers' Library, with Prolegomena.   Oxford, 1895.

Kranich, A.   *Die Ascetik in ihrer dogmatischen Grundlage bei Basilius dem Grossen.*   Paderborn, 1896.

Loofs, F.   *Eustathius von Sebaste.*   Halle, 1898.

Maran.   *Vita Basilii*, prefixed to third vol. of Opera.

Morison, E. F.   "St Basil and Monasticism" (*Church Quarterly Review*).   Oct. 1912.

Morison, E. F.   *St Basil and his Rule.*   Oxford, 1912.

Pargoire, J.   Article "Basile" in *Dictionnaire d'Archéologie chrétienne.*

Schäfer, J.   *Basilius des Grossen Beziehungen zum Abendlande.*   Münster, 1909.

Tillemont.   *Mémoires IX* (2nd ed.).   Paris, 1701—1712.

Venables, E.   Article "Basil" in *Dict. Chr. Biog.*

## Later Greek Monasticism.

Butler, E. C.   Article "Basilian Monks" in *Enc. Brit.* (11th ed.).

Ehrhard, A.   In Krumbacher's *Geschichte der byzantinischen Litteratur.*   Munich, 1897.

Gardner, Miss A.   *Theodore of Studium.*   London, 1905.

Holl, R.   *Enthusiasmus und Bussgewalt.*   Leipzig, 1898.

Lake, K.   *Early Days of Monasticism on Mount Athos.*   Oxford, 1909.

Marin, E.   *Les Moines de Constantinople.*   Paris, 1898.

Meyer, Ph.   *Die Haupturkunden für die Geschichte der Athosklöster.*   Leipzig, 1894.

Riley, A.   *Athos.*   London, 1887.

## Western Monasticism.

Butler, E. C.   *Sancti Benedicti Regula Monachorum.*   Freiburg i.B., 1912.

Dudden, F. H.   *Gregory the Great.*   London, 1905.

Grützmacher, G.   *Die Bedeutung Benedikts von Nursia und seiner Regel in der Geschichte des Mönchtums.*   Berlin, 1892.

Spreitzenhofer, E.   *Die Entwicklung des alten Mönchtums in Italien.*   Vienna, 1894.

# GENERAL INDEX

# INDEX OF MODERN AUTHORS

# INDEX OF PASSAGES OF ANCIENT AUTHORS